ENDORSEMENTS

Hell is real. Unfortunately, most people have little knowledge about this place. Laurie did a remarkable work of explaining the very terrifying details of the unimaginable pain, hopelessness, darkness, judgment, panic, hatred and regret that she experienced when she had a supernatural vision of Hell that changed her life forever. I urge you to read this book and discover for yourself what Hell is really like and how to avoid being there before it's too late.

AARON LAU
Founder, Eternal Investing LLC

My wife and I knew Laurie long before she went to Hell and we have seen a change in her. A seriousness and soberness that, for those who know her, is real!

In my line of work, construction, "Hell" is used to accent a sentence as a cuss word and has been washed down to where it has no real meaning. This book will change that!

BRUCE JACKMAN
President, Forerunner Enterprises Inc.

It is not possible to overstate the importance of the message contained within this book. *The Hell Conspiracy* is a testimony every person needs to read to more clearly understand the gravity of eternity. I cannot more highly recommend this book and its author, Laurie Ditto, with her incredibly timely and vital message!

ANTHONY CAPPOFERRI
Owner, Ariel Logistics

A message about Hell can only have a positive impact upon a person's life if a positive person delivers it. Laurie Ditto exudes positivity, a contagious optimism and a joyful spirit; thus making her a perfect vessel to deliver such weighty content. Laurie is a trustworthy and compassionate guide into a topic many people do not want to address. I am sure that behind every word in *The Hell Conspiracy* is a heart filled with love towards its reader.

AARON SALVATORE
Owner, Providence Pizza

I have known Laurie for a number of years. She has a gift to simply, clearly and directly share God's love. This book captures that truth as well as the pain of Hell and eternal separation from God. She shares a vision unlike any other, an awakening to be shared with everyone!

RON HIATT
President and CEO, U.S. Hay, Inc.

This book and Laurie's testimony is an example of God's love. Laurie is credible, authentic and her heart is to bring people into a restored relationship with the Heavenly Father. Her account of Hell is a sobering reality that is overlooked in today's society. Few have the boldness and confidence to speak truth with love the way Laurie does.

MATTHEW BERTCH
VP of Sales & Marketing, Select Painting

God has given Laurie Ditto a gift which she must share with the world. God's mercy and grace are wonderful for those who will humbly receive it and walk in it. I feel compelled to be more diligent, faithful and watchful every day, knowing that the times are short. I highly recommend *The Hell Conspiracy*.

BRUCE PFUETZE, MD
Kansas

THE HELL
CONSPIRACY

THE HELL CONSPIRACY

An Eye-Witness Account of
Hell, Heaven, and the Afterlife

Laurie A. Ditto

DESTINY IMAGE® PUBLISHERS, INC.
P.O. Box 310, Shippensburg, PA 17257-0310
"Promoting Inspired Lives."

This book and all other Destiny Image and Destiny Image Fiction books are available at Christian bookstores and distributors worldwide.

Cover design by Eileen Rockwell
Interior design by Terry Clifton

For more information on foreign distributors, call 717-532-3040.
Reach us on the Internet: www.destinyimage.com.

ISBN 13 TP: 978-0-7684-4643-2
ISBN 13 eBook: 978-0-7684-4644-9
ISBN 13 HC: 978-0-7684-4646-3
ISBN 13 LP: 978-0-7684-4645-6

For Worldwide Distribution, Printed in the U.S.A.
1 2 3 4 5 6 7 8 / 23 22 21 20 19

DEDICATION

For Jesus, who is able to keep me from stumbling and to present me faultless before the presence of His glory.

CONTENTS

PART 1

HEAVENLY VISION

CHAPTER 1

GIVE ME THAT

Heaven and Hell are eternal. I read about them in the Bible; therefore, their reality is not questionable to me. However, my passion about God, the Bible, Heaven, and Hell have been drastically changed since my spiritual eyes were opened.

I have traveled to Heaven and Hell through visions on different occasions over the last 18 years. This does not make me special, only responsible! Each time I come away with a truth of the Kingdom of Heaven.

Have you ever thought about the Lord's Prayer? It says, "Thy Kingdom come, Thy will be done, on earth as it is in Heaven." I have prayed that prayer for as long as I can remember. It has always made me think about what Heaven must be like.

Things are very different in Heaven. Earth could be so wonderful if we had the principles, practices, wills, and actions of Heaven. It can never be perfect, though, without God Himself. I can never be accused of exaggerating about God's home. It is more wonderfully superb than any mere words I can think of. In the same way, Hell is far worse than the most horrific words that can only begin to portray its inexpressible hideousness.

All people will choose, by how they live on earth, where they spend eternity.

Hell was created for Satan and the demons that rebelled against God. Heaven is where God lives. He desires us to be with Him, but that choice is up to us.

Because I was saved in a vision of Heaven, I would love to share with you about what I saw and experienced while there. This will also allow you to understand me as I reference many Heaven qualities that are not present in Hell.

WHAT IS A PRAYER ROOM?

I learned about a women's conference at the International House of Prayer Kansas City (IHOPKC) from a postcard that somehow came to my home. IHOPKC exists to partner in the Great Commission by advancing 24/7 prayer and proclaiming the beauty of Jesus and His glorious return.

Although at the time I had no interest in doing much of anything due to depression, for some reason I held on to it and knew that I needed to attend. My husband and our two teenage daughters were excited that I wanted to do anything and helped me pack. I drove from my home in upper Michigan to the airport in Minneapolis and hopped a flight down to Kansas City.

When I arrived, I visited the prayer room. I was shocked that such a big name resided in such a small set of trailers. Right away, I walked in with a set of condemning judgments in my mind. I mean, just down the road was a company called International House of Lloyd and they were a huge complex of buildings. It seemed wrong to call that small building the *International* House of Prayer. But really, what did I know about prayer?

Once inside I noticed strange things. Having never been to a prayer room before I didn't know what to expect, but I entered with a set of expectations just the same. In my religious upbringing, I had experienced the orderly conduct of the Catholic Church, the richness of the Word from the Baptist church, and the surprising emotional outbursts of joy from the Pentecostal church. Now to be fair, I never really attended any church often, but I believed that I was going to Heaven because I was a good person.

In the prayer room resided the best of all three churches I had experienced. It seemed to be orderly, very focused on the study of the Bible, and was joyfully spontaneous too. In my judgmental attitude, I could only apply one word—strange.

What I noticed first was that the place was not in a hurry. Going twenty-four hours a day, seven days a week, it oozed patience somehow. There was a worship team playing music up front. The majority of people were in their twenties. I didn't know the words to the songs they sang, but that didn't stop my emotions from engaging. I thought to myself, *I have never heard such happy music.* But it was more than that. I couldn't figure out what felt so different. Those in the room had their eyes closed. I felt like I had stepped into something private and it somehow felt intimate. I thought they all played so well together, but it wasn't performed for me. Like when we attend a concert and the music is performed for the crowd. This music was not like that. Maybe this is what made it seem so intimate. I was deeply moved by the presence in the room, but I could not put my finger on why the presence was so important.

There was a part of the worship where everyone sang their own song to God. I had no idea how something so hectic and individualistic could sound so beautiful. Again, it didn't have anything to do with me, yet somehow I wanted to participate.

When I looked around there were unique things. In my thinking, some fit and some did not. There was a world map. That made sense for the International House of Prayer. People were standing with their hands on the map and rocking back and forth with their eyes closed. This was strange, so it did not fit. There were people at tables working on computers.

The work didn't seem strange, as people do this at a library, but is it okay to do this in a prayer room?

There were people in one area dancing. The dance was rhythmic, but I thought that was strange as there was no one watching the dancers. Some of the dancers waved flags. Strange, who waves flags? (Might I add, I now love to wave flags.) Someone was drawing pictures of Jesus. I figured that would be okay and God would enjoy that.

There were people standing with their hands raised, heads tilted back and tears streaming. Strange. And then there were a few people lying down on the floor crying with their faces in the dirty carpet. Who does this? Strange!

A large part of me wanted to run and get out of the strange room. Well, of course I did. Lost people always want to run from the presence of God.

DRAWN IN

And yet, I was drawn to the music as if I was made out of it or for it. I chose to stay for a while and sat down. There was a lady sitting in the row I chose. She seemed normal. Then the music changed and everyone sang to God their own songs. All of a sudden she was singing in some unknown language.

I remember when I first learned about singing in a strange language. I was a little Catholic kid. My friend was a little Pentecostal kid. I spent a Saturday night at her house. Sunday morning I went to church with her. Her momma found out that I was not baptized in the Holy Ghost. She began dragging me down the aisle toward the front.

At the time I only knew of one good ghost. His name was Casper and all the other ghosts were bad. I was stressed. There was a senior saint on the second row who stopped her and explained that this was not the way to do it and that I was clearly afraid. She put her hand on me and started singing softly with gentle and caring eyes. The song she sang was beautiful and stopped the fear inside of me right away. The name of the song she said was "singing in the spirit." I really liked that song. I liked the lady too.

Later I asked my friend what was wrong with her momma. She told me to do what she does and just say, "I wish I drove a Honda" really fast and her momma would think it was tongues and the Holy Ghost. I decided that I would only ever sleep over again on a Friday night, and she could sleep over at my house on Saturdays.

That experience did something to me. I always wondered about "singing in the spirit" and the gift of tongues. How did it work and was it real? What does the Holy Ghost do? How can a song bring noticeable peace?

Back in the prayer room, I was trying to figure out if this lady was "singing in the spirit." While I listened and hoped that wonderful feeling might return, I heard the voice of God.

He asked, "What do you want?"

And I answered Him immediately, "I want to know if that is real!"

And He did just that. I had the same feeling as when I was a child and that senior saint sang over me. It is very easy to believe in something once God reveals it.

MY LIST

I left the prayer room to drop my things at the hotel and get some food quickly before I headed back to the place where God speaks to people. I was very attracted to the room. It made me feel safe, as if angels or someone was there to help people. I was more comfortable with the idea of angels being there to help me than God.

At that time there was a name it, claim it thing happening in parts of the Body of Christ. My Christian friends tried to explain it to me, but it didn't make much sense that the reason people got stuff was because they claimed it. Now, I thought that obviously I had been wrong. You must just tell God what you want and then you get it.

So, I came back to the prayer room with a short list. This time when God asked me what I wanted I would be more prepared. I wanted a log cabin house on Lake Superior, two four-wheel-drive trucks (I figured since Mike and I both needed a four-by-four and our last name is Ditto, God would understand), and world peace. The world peace was for all of us. I reasoned that there must be something like three wishes, sort of like the genie in the bottle. But if there was already one used on the "singing in the spirit" then I would drop world peace because someone should have asked God for that already. I decided that world peace must be impossible, even for God.

At a certain time, some of the people left the prayer room. I now understand that this happens when the worship set changes. At the time, I assumed that those people must have already gotten from God what they came for.

As I waited, I kept changing seats until finally I was in the front row. I wanted God to see me and talk with me so that I could get the log cabin. But God wasn't talking to me and I started to get upset. Didn't He know I had waited a long time? And what if I had wasted the first wish and it ended up being my only wish?

HEAVEN

In an instant, I was in Heaven standing a distance of maybe 100 yards from Jesus the Christ. My whole brain worked and I had instant recall of everything about my past and things I had learned as well as general facts. The most immediate understanding was that the man standing in front of me was my Creator. I knew I was in His castle. I knew everything in Heaven belonged to Him. I knew that He was the source of all light, the Almighty, that everyone knew Him, that He was very happy and the most powerful being—ever. I also knew that He liked me. I really liked that He liked me. My whole body was electrified in His presence.

He was standing in an archway. I knew it was the Savior. My eyesight was perfect, but it wasn't my eyes that confirmed who He was. Actually, I knew Him better than I know myself. As I looked at Him, He smiled at me. It was so nice to see God happy toward me, but I also understood that He was very holy and I was not.

There really is no way to explain this, but let me try. Jesus turned Himself "on" and "up" for me, like a light going up and down with a dimmer switch. He turned into a Man of unimaginable light. He looked as if He was made out of diamonds or water. He was so sparkly, transparent, and shiny. As He got brighter, it was too difficult for me to look at Him, so I shut my eyes tightly. But His light shone through me somehow.

Jesus didn't want me to shut my eyes, so He turned Himself "down" and I could behold Him. Jesus allowed me to understand that my unique relationship with Him determines the degree of light He can share with me. Also that obedience to Him is considered love, and my love determines the brightness I am capable to behold.

I noticed that He had terrible scars on His wrists from wounds that had healed. I thought that they were in the wrong place. I had always believed the nails had pierced Him in the palms of His hands, not His wrists. Jesus knew my thoughts and didn't stop me to correct my theology. I knew He was after something. I knew that He wanted something from me.

He said, "Laurie, give me that."

I knew Jesus didn't have to ask. If He wanted, He could take whatever. But this God Man was patient. I knew He had many names that identified Him and that He embodied each of those names or attributes perfectly at all times. When Jesus "turned Himself down" so I could gaze on Him, He focused on the attribute I needed the most—patience. I have never met anyone as patient as the Lord. In fact, I first fell in love with His identity of patience.

Again, I knew that He was holy and I was not. I knew I was dark but lovely (see Song of Sol. 1:5). However, the darkness in me was so magnified that I felt paralyzed. Even though everything in me wanted to run to God, I didn't want to get Him dirty. I knew that He wanted the "bad" that was separating us. I panicked. How do you give bad? I thought I was a good person, so what was my bad? The only thing I could think of was cigarette smoking. At the time I smoked three and a half packs of cigarettes a day. I thought that must be it.

Even though I felt I understood what He wanted me to give to Him, I gave the answer I had inside of me. I looked at my feet and said, "No."

I figured that no one gets away with telling God no, but I didn't have a choice. In His presence I knew that I was not able to say yes because the smoking controlled me. I couldn't give away cigarette smoking because it owned me. I waited and waited but nothing happened.

I was sure God would beat someone who didn't obey. I couldn't have been more wrong. When I looked up, He was waiting for me to look. He smiled at me and I realized that He had a plan. It was nothing like I expected. He was nothing like I expected.

He took a step closer to me. When He moved, everything around Him moved. It was fast but very noticeable. My body was drawn to Him and it took me more resistance to remain standing. I longed to be like a child who runs into their parent's arms to apologize, knowing that their parents will love them and it will be okay. But in my deepest heart, I was afraid it would never be okay.

THE PRESENTS

He motioned for me to look into a room. The room had arched openings, like very large windows cut out of the walls, allowing me to gaze inside. There was a doorway arch too, but no door to shut off the room. The castle was built out of rocks, and as I looked into the room I noticed how stunning they were! In fact, everything was magnificent. It was hard not to just stare at one thing because each one was spectacular and fantastically mystical! It made it very hard to focus.

The room was about the size of a basketball court. It had a tall ceiling and was crammed with presents. There were big and little ones with every color wrapping paper you can imagine. I love presents because they signify good things and happy times and these were amazing. I have always enjoyed how well wrapped presents can set the tone for what is to come, and I instinctively knew that these presents were prepared for a person's life. I knew there were several presents per day for someone to open each day of their life. There were many presents from days past that had not yet been opened. I thought to myself that someone was pretty special to Jesus to have a room like that.

The Lord then spoke to my heart and told me that this was my room and that all the presents were for me. He told me that some presents are things He gives and others are things He takes away.

This was too good to be true! How can God have presents all for me and several for every day of my life? I looked at them and was so excited. *Wow!*

I shifted my gaze to Him and saw that He was more excited than me. He had personally chosen these gifts. He asked a second time, "Laurie, give me that."

I wanted to say yes but I just couldn't. Then I was filled with the why of not giving it to Him. I had tried to stop smoking before but I could not. *And,* I knew that if I stopped smoking, I would get fat. I mean, husbands leave for all kinds of reasons, right? Isn't one that the wife got fat? I didn't know which reason Mike was going to choose, but it wasn't going to be that one. I waited and waited. Surely this time God would beat me. But nothing happened. When I finally looked up, He was again waiting patiently for me. What a patient Man, so unlike anyone I knew. He was smiling at me. How could He smile? Everything in me wanted to smile back, but as an adult I have trained myself to keep a straight face in stressful situations.

He took a step closer. When He moved, He changed everything! There is no real way to explain this. It is as if Jesus were standing on the moon and took one step toward us on Earth and the distance traveled in that one step was the distance between the moon and Earth. When He moved one step, He traveled a great distance and many things changed.

DIVINE DANCE

Then, He turned His being into light and invited me to look inside of Him. This is hard to explain, but it was as if He became a TV. I watched a memory or a future event from His heart play out on His lighted Being. He was showing me something important for us both.

I watched Jesus dancing with a woman. She was His bride.

He wore amazing clothes like none I have ever seen, or maybe it is true that the man makes the suit. No man has ever looked as wonderful as Him. His suit fit Him perfectly. It had gold buttons, which were a sign of the highest form of respect. Only Jesus is worthy to wear these buttons.

The clothes in Heaven are supernatural. Imagine that all the colors ever made, including the exceptional and breathtaking colors only found in Heaven, were compressed together to make something like a dot or a sequin. That sequin was unique because it was every color working perfectly in unity, and as such it created light. Jesus dressed His people in this material.

The bride was wearing an empire waist dress made out of this heavenly material. It had puffy little sleeves that covered the top part of her shoulders and a higher scooped neckline. The dress had a lot of material flowing from the drop line so it fanned out gracefully with each turn. And she danced barefooted.

I watched as their eyes met. His eyes were like a fire. This is hard to explain, but Jesus' eyes move and are alive in a different way, like a campfire. Have you ever watched a campfire and when the logs move you realize that while you were staring time went on? When we look into His eyes, nothing else matters.

When the bride turned from Him in a soft, slow twirl, darkness would try to touch the hem of her dress. The fire in His eyes shifted and a very serious and frightful look caused the darkness to flee from her. The fire in His eyes forced the darkness away, and she never had a clue about that fire. He loved her with everything He had. She was the most important thing ever to Him.

I watched and watched. As I did, something was going on inside of me. I hurt! I wanted Jesus to look at me with those eyes of fire. I wanted it so badly that there was an ache deep down inside of me. I didn't want to live unless Jesus looked at me that way. I wanted to be the beautiful godly woman who had made everything about herself special for Jesus.

This woman was perfect. She had made herself that way in obedient love. She could behold Him in His great light. Then I noticed her feet and her ankles. I looked again to be sure. Could this be? Yes, she was me! Those ankles were mine. My heart exploded! Jesus loved me! I didn't recognize her at first because I was not like her yet. But after seeing her dance, I understood that I *could* be like her. I wanted, no needed, to be her.

I said, "*Yes!*" Yes, I want to give Jesus everything to make me into that woman.

In that minute I understood what He wanted. It was more than just the bad, it was me. Without Him, I am bad. He wanted my whole heart— all the parts that were lovely and unlovely. He could have commanded the addiction of cigarettes to leave because I needed help. But He needed me to desire Him in my choice. I needed to trust Him. I moved toward Him and He moved toward me. I knew that *everything* around me was moving and changing.

He put His forehead to my forehead. In that amazing gesture, things started happening. He began to rewrite my belief system about myself. He gave me something better than self-esteem; it was Christ-esteem. I was no longer suicidal, in need of medicine, craving cigarettes, or depressed. I was His! I was whole, special, needed, important, wanted, and loved. I was His favorite!

His presence was so captivating that He kept me in that place until I was filled with the love and assurance and all that He desired for me. I know that He put many thoughts, plans, purposes, and tasks in me. But more than this, He put who I am inside of me.

Go

I was prepared and equipped. I was ready to live as a child of God. I asked Him, "Is there anything I can do for You?"

He answered, "Go, tell others about Me."

At first I am sure it appears that He answered a question, but I know that His answer was to the question I should have asked instead: "Who am I?"

I left the vision and was back in the prayer room. I was a new me!

I was different and new when I went home. Mike liked that I was so happy, sort of. He didn't like that I insisted that he and our daughters listen again and again about Heaven and how I am Jesus' favorite one.

They didn't like that now I was bossy and pushy, wanting everything to be what Jesus would like. I had to buy a Bible and read my Bible and listen to every radio program about God. I had to be at church as much as I could because I had to catch up. I knew that God had presents for me that I hadn't opened yet. And in catching up, I was sure that I could open those ones from days past because I needed to be that bride dancing with Jesus.

I began telling everyone about Jesus. I still do.

My family was stressed out when I got saved. We had known religious fanatics and had stayed away from them. Now, according to them, I was one. My family was divided—me against three. But I knew that if I prayed for the Kingdom to come, something good must happen.

Mike was not sure about what had happened to me, so he wanted to take me back to IHOPKC so I could see that I had misunderstood them. He thought that people do not become that radical because of Jesus. I was very excited that he was going to bring me back there.

Mike met Jesus while at IHOPKC. It was his own experience where he knew that Jesus was real and worthy to be worshiped in everything we do. Mike immediately became Mr. Radical.

When we returned home from this trip, Mike spoke with our daughters. Their response to him was "Dad, you were supposed to fix her, not become like her!" Our family was still divided. It was now parents against children. The girls fought going to church, prayer time, and youth group. They stuck together like glue against anything that seemed "religious."

That winter IHOPKC was hosting the first Onething conference. Mike bribed our daughters to go by promising them an airplane ticket (they had never flown), staying at the nice hotels, eating out at fancy restaurants, and a $300 shopping spree each. They knew Dad had lost his mind because he is naturally a very frugal man. They agreed to put up with four days of "Mom and Dad's God fantasy" for the fringe benefits.

On the first night of the conference both of our daughters experienced a healing in their bodies. Our youngest daughter instantly gave her life to the Lord. She felt Him and knew that He was real. Even though both daughters were healed, our oldest daughter ran as fast as she could toward the darkness. It was now three against one in our family. And we three prayed every day for the one.

The following year, Mike asked our oldest to come again to the Onething conference. She refused. He sweetened the pot. He invited her two dearest friends to come along and said he would cover their plane tickets, hotels, and food. Our daughter said absolutely not. We kept praying to our Great God who answers prayers.

Surprise, all three girls came to the conference and each one gave their lives to Jesus. People say, "You bribed your children!" as if it is a bad thing.

Mike says that he can't think of a better way to spend his money than to put people in the presence of Jesus and let Him love on them so they can choose the God who desires them.

In our overwhelming thankfulness to Jesus, we poured ourselves into church, the youth group, and our children. We took the majority of our vacations to visit the International House of Prayer, where we fell more in love with our God. Imagine our surprise when we were invited by Him to move to Kansas City.

OBEDIENCE

Choosing Jesus is the first, most important decision we make. I am so grateful to the Holy Spirit for teaching us how to pray and prompting us to pray often. I am eternally grateful that Jesus is the Lord of our lives.

Jesus remaining Lord of our lives, however, is up to us. Obedience is not only important but it is essential. I read the Bible. I believed in Heaven and Hell. I understood that loving Jesus meant obeying Him. But I ignored His promptings and warning visions about the seriousness of the unforgiveness that was in my heart.

PART 2

VISION OF HELL

CHAPTER 2

THE HELL CONSPIRACY INTRODUCED

Have you ever been a part of a conspiracy?

Years ago our family hosted a weekly game night on Fridays and Saturdays, where we opened our home for our daughters and their friends to hang out and play games. This allowed a safe and drug-free environment. To the kids' delight, it included free pop, pizza, chips, candy and a winning jackpot of money that could be used to fill their gas tanks.

There was a young man, Tim who always wanted to play a specific game. He was bright, calculating, funny and great to be around. Unless he was playing THAT game. It wasn't just that he was good at the game; it was that he was so prideful, haughty and negative when he played. He would do whatever it took to win. Those negative traits seemed to increase in him as the weeks went by and began spilling out of game night and ruining his relationships.

I devised a conspiracy—to help him.

I contacted everyone before the game night and explained that we were going to do one thing that night—beat Tim. I explained that it didn't matter who won so long as Tim lost. Everyone agreed.

The game we devised made no sense to Tim. He couldn't figure out why people did what they did. No one but Tim was trying to win. When Tim finally lost, I shared that the game had been rigged. Tim was incredibly hurt and angry. He felt betrayed and manipulated which is exactly how someone would feel being on that side of a conspiracy.

We all told Tim how much we love him and what a great guy he was outside of game night. Tim agreed that something would come over him when he played. He couldn't identify the sin until we brought it to his attention. He just knew that no matter what, or how, he HAD to win at all costs. After our little conspiracy, he identified the pattern and he was able to change. This conspiracy resulted in a positive outcome but, understand, it was a conspiracy designed for a positive outcome.

By nature, a conspiracy is not positive.

There is a Hell Conspiracy. It takes place on the game board of life and everyone is playing. It includes opinions, distorted facts, altered history, fracturing religions, unethical politics, death and who controls life. There are also very real players that we cannot see who understand the game from a vantage point we cannot easily obtain.

The Hell Conspiracy is the biggest and most costly deception on the face of the earth that lulls countless people into indifference. Evil has formulated shortcuts and all-encompassing false realities to pacify the ticking clock.

In Hell, the conspiracy had revealed my sin nature as I believed I was there to stay. But, like Tim's change, my change was to become a watchman and sound an alarm to restore my relationship with God and then warn others.

The Hell Conspiracy has many facets. Of course it would, being the longest playing deception ever. Be assured, you have encountered many of the controversies and nuances during your lifetime.

If we could outline this age-old plot it would include uncountable, multi-layered tiers of deception designed to discredit the very existence of Hell and all of the supernatural. The Creator of Hell would have to be defamed and disgraced along with anyone who believes in its existence. Other gods would have to be created along with a multitude of confusing rules, regulations and belief systems ultimately leading to the construction of atheism. Each false belief system would need false prophets, exposed lies and shameful greed to ensure a foul stench toward the topic of any religion.

In this plot, there would have to be a breaking down of family and its values, truth, morality and absolutes to allow for the coveted independent belief structures. Pride and haughtiness would be seen as assets and necessities for leadership. Winning, no matter the cost, would be positively legitimate and absolutely encouraged. Obedience would be a ridiculous, childish attribute.

Loyalty, dependability, righteousness and holiness would have to be defined inside of the confines of humanitarian acts that could be manipulated by the controlling leader. This would produce leaders who are above accountability.

Godly words and understandings would have to be recalculated. There could not be a definition of things created such as right or wrong, marriage between a man and a woman, and even male or female.

The Hell Conspiracy has been going on since before the Garden of Eden. Fortunately, the Maker of Hell, who is the Lord God Almighty, didn't create Hell for you and me. The Lord God is desperate to bring His clarity and direction to allow us to win this conspiracy set-up.

I experienced a supernatural vision of Hell that has clarified my understanding of the Hell Conspiracy. I believe this account will give the texture and substance needed to hear the urgency of the alarm I am sounding.

CHAPTER 3

HELL OPENS

THE MEETING

It is important to share that I am taking the next five chapters to explain something that happened instantly. It wasn't an orderly progression, but I've tried to lay it out in an orderly fashion here.

It was Thursday, August 28, 2008.

In a vision, Jesus took me to Hell. It was like a terrible, life-changing accident. You know how when an accident happens, you keep replaying over in your mind what you could have done differently? I have replayed August 28th over and over at least 1,000 times, if not more. "Oh God, what did I do wrong? Why did this happen to me?"

Because I have looked at this "accident" so much, I know many little details that have been etched into my memory. Many of them are unimportant, but I have memorized them nonetheless. I have looked for every little decision or detail that resulted in the worst day of my entire life—and possibly the most life-giving day for me.

I woke early that Thursday morning filled with a fresh hunger for the Word of God and to see the fullness of the gifts of healing manifested in my life. I desired to touch God in a fresh way. It was as if a new light or level of expectancy had been opened to me. The day before, I had been in a marvelous prayer meeting with a couple from England. We were gripped with intercession for the great city of London. In the 60-minute prayer time, I felt as if God wanted to do great things amidst the darkness in that nation. I had a new longing to see the city and declare the goodness of our great King there. I desired for people I had never met to encounter God in a desperate way, and I kept thinking about the possibility of taking a trip to preach on this important city's streets. Maybe I was going on a trip soon?

I got around quickly and lightheartedly that Thursday morning. Singing, happy, in love with my family, my life, and the world. Everything seemed perfect. Better than perfect.

I worked for the evangelism department at the International House of Prayer, now called the Kansas City Evangelists' Fellowship (KCEF). That morning we were in our weekly two-hour evangelism meeting. The structure of the meeting had three parts. First, a time of worship to draw near to the Father. Then, testimonies from the workers of the harvest. Finally, a time of teaching or exhortation by a speaker. This meeting had always been one of my favorites because it strengthened and connected me with others for encouragement and fellowship.

I arrived early to help set up the meeting space. When I first walked into the KCEF meeting room, I knew that God's angels were there. I listened to the worship team practice, but something felt different from normal. I had a wonderful sense that even the worship practice was going to take me into a place of connecting with Jesus. Excitement filled me about the possibility of joining with God so closely for a second day in a row.

I had forgotten a CD for recording the meeting, so I ran back to my office. I hurried because I knew that this was going to be a great meeting and I didn't want to miss anything. What if Jesus was coming to the meeting and what if something very powerful was going to happen?

I told my boss upon returning from my office to expect something wonderful. He had asked me to let him know when I felt supernatural things because we all want to grow in our understanding of the supernatural. He said that he could feel that the worship practice had something extra on it, as if it was already the worship service.

I continued thinking that something fantastic was going to happen. I desired to see God stretch out His arms and fill our meeting with signs and wonders. I believe the Bible is true when it says that blind eyes should see, deaf ears should hear, and the dead should be raised. I believe that Jesus means what He says and that we're supposed to do the things He did—even greater things than these. So I was excited as I felt angels coming from all around the area to be a part of what was about to happen.

As the meeting began with worship, I was standing at the back of the room. I stood back there to assist my boss if he needed something. Also, I chose to stand at the back because I like to worship God. I get self-conscious when I think people are looking at me, but at the back of the room those thoughts don't enter my mind.

Before I can enter into worship in a heart-connect way, let alone in spirit and truth (see John 4:24), I have to tell my body, *You will worship God*. So that day I raised my hands to God and I sung loudly to Him. I engaged my mind to worship Jesus by contemplating the beauty of His love and the magnificence of His dying on the cross for me. I let my emotions worship Him, which allows my heart to open to Him.

The worship leader was helping us pray for our lost family members, friends, neighbors, and co-workers. To really get a sustained heart for lost people, I have found I have to make it personal. I have to truly think about what it would be like for my lost family members to not make it to Heaven. When we think about someone we love not being in Heaven, it creates a real sadness and if we think about it long enough, it creates a desperation.

These thoughts allow us to identify with a real emotion for the people we love. Because it's such a negative emotion to experience, most people don't go there. Evangelists are willing to expose their hearts to let God's truth and urgency shape us. We don't like the down emotion either, but by allowing it we become more tender to the eternal truth for lost souls. Then, sharing about Jesus becomes essential and very personal.

As we sang an evangelistic song, I felt the presence of holiness come into the room. The song gripped me and just seemed to add to the excitement I already felt. The music was captivating and took me to what I will call a worship place. Do you know the frustration when you are worshiping Jesus and someone interrupts you to ask a question? But you were in a special place with God and you had to come away from there into the right now because of the interruption? I was in that uninterrupted worship place, wondering what God was doing. Wondering who He was going to visit.

I remember hoping that when He was done with whomever, He would also encounter me. The feeling in the room was the same as other times that I had been invited to come away with the Lord to visit Heaven. I knew I was being invited to go in the spirit. The holiness had come for me. I said, "Yes."

HELL OPENS

Then, all of a sudden, the front of the room opened up. I instantly opened my eyes and saw the transformation as it happened. The Hell realm unlocked and I heard massive gates creak open and I felt extreme heat enter the room. I looked with my eyes wide open and I saw Hell through the gates. I saw it! I was shocked that it was right there. Wasn't it supposed to be in the center of the earth or below us? To say I panicked is an understatement!

Worship and prayer continued around me. The people were oblivious that Hell was at the front of the room. I watched those ominous gates open as I watched the people worshiping. The two places, the meeting room and Hell were together.

I frantically looked to see who might help me. The others didn't see the gates, hear that sound, or feel the heat. Instinctively, I started screaming. I felt the sound of fear coming from my own body. I knew that my spirit was being demanded to submit. As I screamed, my spirit was also making a sound that deeply hurt my heart and brain while it also panicked every blood cell in my body.

Something came flying past the gates of Hell. It was coming for me. It was like an arm without fingers that grabbed me and sucked me into Hell. The arm was very powerful. It was attached to me like a suction cup in the area of my chest and began dragging me further into Hell. As quickly as it shot out from Hell, it just as quickly moved back. I tried to pull back and break the hold it had on me but it was too powerful.

Before I could blink, I knew this—it was too late. The gates slammed shut with a terrible sound of finality. I knew there was no man on this side or that who could ever open those gates. Only Jesus could because He owns Hell.

THE OCEAN PROBLEM

Let me stop here to explain something. I want you, the reader, to understand the problem that I face. Trying to explain Hell is beyond difficult! It is like describing the ocean to someone who has never seen it. And let's say that, with my limited ability or resources, I tried to describe the ocean by picking up a glass of water and saying, "This is like the ocean, but the ocean is different." You would tell me that the glass of water is nothing like the ocean.

I would then try to explain some of the differences between the ocean and the glass of water:

- You can't see where the ocean begins and where it ends with your eye.

- The temperature of the ocean is always changing.

- The ocean is always moving.

- There are things that live in the ocean that are much bigger than the amount of water in the glass.

- The ocean is extra salty, not at all like the kind of water in the glass.

- The ocean has depths that we can't reach.

And the list goes on and on.

But to understand the ocean from my perspective you would have to at least try to see that the ocean is like the glass of water.

There are simply no earthly words to describe Hell because there is *nothing* like it in any culture in the world. This is the problem that I have in trying to explain what Hell is like. I must use earth words that are wrapped in the midst of grace, mercy, and love because God has left these precious qualities on the earth.

My limited vocabulary is also an issue, as well as the fact that the memories of indescribable torture make me near speechless to explain what I felt and saw. I am positive that the words that I am using cannot do justice to even a tiny portion of the horrific state of Hell.

Hell is a place without God. I understand that people shut down at the thought of no God in Hell, but let me explain before you write this all off. Only the judgments of God reside in Hell. Although the Bible says, "If I make my bed in Hell, behold, You are there" (Ps. 139:8), it isn't saying that God is in Hell, only that He is God even over that place. In Hell the judgments of God are so huge and eternal and in perfect control of the righteousness. However, nothing good exists in Hell. It's not like I could catch God's eye and He would have mercy. If we believe God is in

Hell, then the Devil is able to cloud the truth and we will believe that Hell doesn't exist, that no one perishes or that we can pray someone's way out of Hell. For those who do not receive Jesus Christ as their Savior, death results in everlasting punishment and eternal separation from God (see 2 Thess. 1:7-9). It should terrify us that people we know are going where there is no God. If we get this, then we will know holy fear and actually desire to live a holy life.

I can never lie about how terrible Hell is because even my best description is only a fragment of the inexpressible agony. I can never exaggerate in any way the pain, suffering, fear, loneliness, or exile. It is categorically beyond anything my words can portray.

I have tried to expand my vocabulary to look for words that could express the realities of Hell in hopes of saving someone from going there. But they all fail to reach the full understanding of its horror.

There is no worse place *anywhere!* It is an area God made for things that God does not want with Him. Those are the Devil and his demons, according to the Bible (see Matt. 25:41). Hell was not created for mankind and the earth is nothing like Hell! And I need to be clear that there is no way to live in Hell while on earth, no matter what anyone says. There is no comparison between the worst things on the earth and the mildest events in Hell.

Imagine if there is a secret door that leads into another world. When I was a little girl I watched *The Wizard of Oz*. The beginning of that movie is in black and white, and all of a sudden when Dorothy walked out of the house everything was in living color. It looked so brilliantly strange and was confusing and unrecognizable. While the place was exciting and adventuresome, all she wanted was to go home. Now imagine if she arrived in Oz and what snatched her was an inexpressible dark, torturous terror. And imagine if she knew there was absolutely no way to get home, ever. In a very minor way, Hell is like a negative Oz.

I Am in Hell

I passed through gates that trapped the darkness inside. The first thing I knew when I got there: I was in Hell.

I remember once traveling and when I woke up in the night looking around I was disoriented and I couldn't remember where I was. In the few nanoseconds as I tried to get my bearings, I felt panicked. Once my memory of the past, yesterday, caught up, I remembered where I was and everything was okay. Our past is a part of what makes us who we are and gives us a grounding point. Without it we are at the mercy of someone to tell us who we are. As I was leaving earth I felt my good past and the goodness from my life leave me or stay behind. It was blocked and all that remained was the bad past.

The realization that I was in Hell was unquestionably shocking and beyond hurtful! I don't know how to explain just how panicked I was, although you may understand a bit if you've ever been lost. I remember when I was a child and my family went to Toronto, Canada on vacation. We had never been there. We wanted to see the city and decided that the subway was the way to travel. We waited on the platform for the train. It arrived and the doors opened. Half of us got on the train, the door closed, and half of us were left on the platform. And this was back before anyone had cell phones.

I remember the panic as the subway train took off and I wondered what would happen to us. I remember looking through the glass at my mom who was not on the train with me as she held my little sister's hand while I was whisked away from her. My dad was trying to tell her that he would get off at the first stop but where was that? It was a sinking, eerie, and stomach-upsetting moment. I knew I couldn't fix the problem and there was nothing I could do to change the situation. There was nothing anyone could do. I tried to process, wondering which one of us was lost. Them or me? And what was the plan? From the perspective of a child there is no good plan. And then the panic gripped my heart. *What are we going to do?*

It was like this but more dire. I was like a child and I had no plan. I had stepped onto a subway going to Hell and no one else got on. It only went one place and no one ever wants to go there. I was going to Hell and I was the lost one. I panicked like no other panic I have ever experienced in my entire life. In fact, I knew that if I could add up every panic I have ever felt, it didn't come close to what I was experiencing.

Someone said to me, "Laurie, you are in Hell!"

"Oh my God!" I answered.

I knew many things all at once. As I break them down to explain each one individually, it gives the false appearance that it was a slow progressive onslaught. But everything was immediate. For the sake of explanation, I knew three things first—I was in Hell, eternally, for unforgiveness.

Once the understanding of the judgment arrived in my heart there were five distinct pains:

1. Water—Immediately, all the water left my body, creating a desperate, painful need.

2. Bone marrow—In an instant my bones turned black.

3. Breath—The first breath allowed fire to touch everything in me and be carried throughout my body.

4. Agreement—Agreeing with the judgement that Hell is where I belonged removed my humanity.

5. The Garment—I will share more on this later.

Before that day, I had not studied much about Hell. I believed it was real because I believe the whole Bible is true, but I didn't think that anybody like me would ever go there. I also knew about the Bible's stance on unforgiveness. Although I knew, it was just easier to hold on to unforgiveness. I mean, with time, unforgiveness had become part of me. I would never have thought unforgiveness could take a person to Hell. My view was swiftly changed.

CHAPTER 4

RIGHTEOUS HELL

KNOWING

My whole brain started working as I was being sucked out of the room. I had the ability to remember everything. Every minute of every day that I had ever lived. I could have told you things like what was in our refrigerator on any given day, every time I got angry with people in traffic and every hurtful word ever said to me. Events and details that seemed impossible to remember but as I was leaving this earthly realm for that one of Hell, my brain came fully alive and I used it to 100 percent capacity.

The Bible says God the Father knows all the hairs on your head (see Matt. 10:30). When I read that, I wondered how it is possible for Him to know the number of hairs on my head. It's because God knows everything. His brain is much bigger, stronger, smarter, and more capable than mine.

In Hell, I knew things like this. I knew and understood the Bible perfectly. Every word of God that I had ever read was now completely clear. And I knew exactly how much I had disobeyed in comparison to my biblical understanding. I was keenly aware of everything about myself and my body. Stuff like my blood moving, my eyes seeing, and how all the parts of my body work. I have never been in such awe of the creation of a human body. Everything I learned in eighth grade science I recalled perfectly. But even more, a supernatural knowledge filled in the blanks that I did not already know.

My knowledge about Hell, from the Scriptures, was also at the front of my awareness. I knew that everything I had read was true. All heartbreakingly true. I knew all of the scriptures on Hell, how much information was provided to me in the Bible about it, and how those scriptures fit with the rest of the Bible. I was fully awakened to the terrible reality of this place. The panic of knowing that I was in Hell grew. I was not a visitor.

GOD IS NOT BAD

I understood that Hell is a relational issue, not a problem to solve like a math question. A person cannot get out of Hell if they acquire the right answer. Hell was created because of a relational issue. An angel refused to love God! One of the most important things that I had divine understanding of is that Hell wasn't created because of human sin and we don't go to Hell because of one particular sin. We all have sinned (see Rom. 3:23). This isn't just a sin issue. It is a relational issue. Because of the Devil and his disobedience, disrespect, and disregard of God, Hell was created.

Let me say it a different way. Satan knew the Trinity. He was a servant created along with all the angels. He chose to rebel and attempted a takeover of Heaven with his disregard for God. Satan convinced a third of the angels to rebel with him. Hell was created for **this** relational issue. There is power in disobedience, disrespect, and disregard. Those attitudes and actions required that the Father create a place for them. Hell is filled with that darkness.

We think someone goes to Hell because they sinned, but really it is about disobeying and disrespecting God. The Bible says, *"Kiss the Son, lest He be angry, and you perish in the way"* (Ps. 2:12). That kiss is about love, affection, and obedience. We mistakenly think that because people mess up, God sends them to Hell. But that is not true. How can we think God is bad? As if to say that we are kinder, more loving, gentler, or more understanding that Him? People go to Hell because they refuse to be in a heart-transforming relationship with God. Hell is about a refusal to love God and have a relationship based on His requirements.

Although God literally forgave me everything, when I gave my life to Him, I refused to choose to forgive *certain* ones. I was just like the unmerciful servant in one of Jesus' parables (see Matt. 18:21-35).

In the parable Jesus told, He desired to expand His disciples' understanding of forgiveness from Heaven's perspective. A servant owed a king more debt than he could ever fully pay in several lifetimes. The servant asked the king to be patient with him and he would pay back every penny. The king is no idiot. He knows the servant will never be able to pay it back.

The king offers the man an incredible gift and cancels his debt.

The servant leaves the presence of the king and bumps into a man who owes him a day's wages. The servant demands full payment immediately. The man asks the servant to be patient with him. When the man cannot pay, the servant has him thrown in jail.

The king hears about it and asks his servant why he who was forgiven everything didn't turn around and forgive. The king calls him wicked and reinstates the servant's entire debt.

When the king forgave the wicked servant's debt, he offered the servant a relationship and a way of life that included mercy, grace, and forgiveness. When the servant accepted the gift, he received far more than just the debt cancellation. When the servant refused to show the same mercy, grace, and forgiveness to the man who owed him a day's wage, it was proof that he had rejected the king's gift.

The servant refused to enter into the relationship of mercy, grace, and obedience to the king. If he had, he would have acted like the king and repeated the same gesture. The real gift offered to the servant was a piece of the king's heart, not the money.

Jesus said at the end of the parable something that made my situation in Hell very dire. He said, "*So also my heavenly Father will do to every one of you, if you do not forgive your brother from your heart.*" (Matt.18:35 ESV).

We start out loving God because He loves us, but then we love Him because of everything we *know* about Him as we go deeper and deeper into relationship. Marriages don't end because someone cheated. The end starts way before that cheating when the couple won't be in relationship with one another. So how much more is that true about Jesus? There is mercy when we mess up. But we reject His mercy when we defiantly harden our hearts (see Heb. 4:7). The Bible teaches that God longs to be gracious to us . In the same way that it takes a repentant heart to receive salvation, it takes a repentant heart to receive mercy. Hell is where those who refuse God will find themselves.

This never made sense to me before, but it is the most important lesson I learned there. Hell was created because Satan didn't want relationship with God and demanded his glory from Him. Satan would not love God. He, in fact, hated God. So God created a place for Satan, but there is no glory there; there is no love there. There is only pain apart from Jesus. God loves and wants all of His creation with Him, but not all of His creation loves or wants Him. This is where I was and this is where I was going to be, forever. And it was always going to be like this. I had rejected God and His ways. Not all of my sin took me to Hell. I was in Hell because of unforgiveness. I was in Hell because I refused to receive love and let that love change me. I went to Hell because what Jesus said would happen, happened (see Matt. 6:12-15; 18:21-35; Mark 11:25-26).

I hated the ways that I had lived on the earth. I hated that I had been born. *Hate* is everywhere in Hell, and I was just beginning to see the depths of hate as it began to fill and overtake me.

I knew why I was in Hell. I knew that I was in Hell because I had not forgiven certain people. I refused to free them. Not that I couldn't forgive, because we can all forgive. It was because I chose not to forgive them. There were no thoughts of negotiating my sentence, as if God had mistakenly picked the wrong girl.

On the earth, when somebody comes to tell me that I am guilty of this or that, I want to hold a meeting and give my side of the story. This is good because we really need much better communication. I have been in many different situations where I told the absolute true facts as I recalled them while someone else did the same thing, yet we had a conflict between us. Which one of us is a liar? Neither of us. We are trying to tell the truth based on facts according to our personal perspectives.

In Hell I already knew the complete truth from God's perspective. The ways of God are righteous, always righteous! Even though I wished it were not so, I knew that it was. The judgment of God is true. Everyone knows that truth there. The judgment of me being in Hell eternally for not forgiving people on the earth was completely righteous. In my own knowledge, being in Hell was completely righteous. I can't tell you what that did to me then, or the soberness that it puts in me even today. It's not like on the earth where innocent people have gone to jail for something they didn't do. That never happens in Hell. Everyone in Hell is there because they are guilty. Because they would not love and obey God. For me to try to explain this any further is like the ocean problem.

It takes me a lot of words to try and explain what I experienced in Hell because, as I said, there are not adequate words to describe that place. It's like trying to interpret from one language to another language. Sometimes one word takes sentences to explain because there is literally no word in the other language that compares. Sitting here in the presence of God trying to write to you about the language of a place where there is no God is seemingly impossible. There are words and emotions that are reserved only for Hell. Everything about where the presence of God and His goodness are is in direct conflict with Hell; where He is not. Trying to interpret that for you is the ocean problem, but now that ocean problem is growing.

As I faced the reality of my judgment, I was in overload. I was inundated with an ever-increasing fear and knowledge that Hell is not only everything that I had read in the Bible but so much worse. But there is no overload shut-down mechanism in Hell. No shutting off, no taking a break, no passing out, and no quitting. The horribleness and pain in Hell accelerated and continued to get worse. I was literally experiencing inside my body the truth I had read in the Bible. I was eternally damaged!

PAIN AND REGRET

My body in Hell was real. Some have the idea that maybe we cease to exist when we leave the earth. This is wrong. We don't disappear or turn into a fog when we leave the earth. I was still me and my body still had every sense intact—sight, sound, taste, smell, and touch. My body would experience every horrible punishment, eternally. The knowledge that I was trapped in Hell and that God was not there escalated the fear and pain inside my body. That pain and fear never stopped growing the entire time I was there. I was plagued with issues such as stomach cramps, extreme shaking in my legs and arms, vomiting, retching, and so much more. They all felt the same as here but much more intense because no one can provide help or comfort and there is no hope of it ever changing or getting better.

Quickly, I realized that my body was not important there. I didn't appreciate the importance of my body on the earth until I understood it wasn't at all important in Hell. On earth, our bodies are the vessel to carry the presence of God, and that makes them special and important. Our bodies were made in the image of God and are, therefore, like God.

In Hell my body changed shape. Without the goodness of God and with the judgment of God, I could no longer be in His image. And the transformation of my body into what it became was excruciating.

In Hell, there is no do-over or second time around the mountain because being in Hell is final. The game is over and we have chosen to be a loser.

As I realized this, I was overcome by eternal regret, which only grew. I was keenly aware of time passing. I started wishing it was a minute ago because I understood with each passing second that everything was getting worse. I was very quickly being brought up to speed to be equal with what was going on in Hell, and with each passing second the magnitude of everything ramped up. It was overwhelming a second ago. But it became far worse a second later, and I literally have no language to express how it could get any worse than horrific.

The only example I have is of a union worker who started at his job 20 years ago making a dollar an hour. However, today if someone jumped into that job they start at $50 an hour. It was like that. Maybe it would have been slower if I had been to Hell 20 years ago, but on the day that I arrived, it was like I was being rushed to catch up to all this pain because a more terrifying day was coming. It was right up ahead. Everything was racing toward the end where the maximum amount of pain was waiting. When I arrived in Hell, I didn't get the time to slowly accept the terribleness. I just had to be a part of the new normal pain level.

The pain of regret is a distinctive pain. It was devastating because I knew I didn't have to be there. However, because it was too late to change anything, unimaginable regret became a part of me. Regret is all the more terrible when the cause cannot be fixed. But in Hell, there is never a chance to make it better, so I had to live with it forever.

Additionally, regret is completely consuming there because it has touched *everything*. On the earth, it is limited to an individual relationship or a time period in our past. But in Hell, regret has no constraints. I regretted that I wasn't in relationship with Jesus and I couldn't get away from all the bad stuff I had done. I could only see the bad stuff (remember, all the good left me when I arrived). I had this new identity of regret, which made me a monster in my own eyes. On earth, even though I had low self-esteem and self-respect, even at my darkest time when I was suicidal, there was still an element of value in me. But now all of my value had been weighed out and found lacking. I had a new identity of zero value. This is a sickness or disease you can only get in Hell. It isn't like mental illness; it is Hell illness. Anytime we live with regret, it kills a part of us.

For instance, when I was a little girl, my grandfather used to tell me it would take a very special man to marry me. When I met and married my husband, my grandfather couldn't come to the wedding. After we got married, he kept asking me when I was going to bring that boy to meet him. In a little over eight months, he was dead and I never got to introduce Mike to one of the men in my life whom I loved so much. There was a regret in me—*why hadn't I made time? Wasn't he important enough that he deserved for us to take a trip, whatever the cost?* That regret still hurts me. I wonder what he would have said about Mike, and I would have loved for Mike to have met him so that I could share and connect with Mike about my beloved grandfather. But that is never going to happen. And that time period of my life, even though it has been over 35 years, still hurts. We all have regrets. In Hell I had a never-ending onslaught of crushing regrets every moment.

My mind was on a wheel and I kept replaying the facts:

- Because of sin, I am in Hell eternally. Regret!
- Because of unforgiveness, I am in Hell eternally! Increased regret!
- I knew unforgiveness was sin, but I lived it anyway! Regret was my life forever.

THE FLAME

I was suspended over something that was bubbling. It was black and bubbling and it went as far as I could see. I was higher than many, so I wasn't as close to that bubbling heat as some.

I tried to get my bearings as much as I could in Hell. I tried to get my brain to slow down. I understood that I was suspended in a tear-dropped flame cell that was created out of the building materials of Hell such as fear and darkness. Doesn't it make sense that we would be trapped in a tear drop? Like God didn't do everything for us? I'm sure Jesus was weeping that I was in Hell.

I was trapped and isolated in all this darkness, in all this fear. It just had me. There were no thoughts of escaping. I was literally wrapped in fear as it wound itself around me. Not up against me but enfolding me as it seeped into my cell like smoke. I was trapped in a cocoon of fear that began to block any view out of my prison. It was isolating me in a wicked way. It took me just a few minutes or maybe it was only seconds to realize that I would never get to anyone else. I would be in Hell by myself, because being near someone else was a form of comfort, which is not allowed in Hell.

The atmosphere was a fog comprised of multiple layers of blackness because there is no light in Hell. Jesus is light and He's not there.

I longed for a drink of water as I felt the drying up of my bones. There was no more water in my body. I could not have water in Hell because water is a source of life. There is no life there. There is only death.

My body started contorting, trying to find relief from the agonizing pain in the flame. My bones were grinding against bones. I watched the marrow in my left arm turn from healthy yellow to deathly black. I knew this was happening all over my body. That marrow is what gives us life, but nothing of life is allowed in Hell. I hated that I chose this. I was stuck in the flame forever and there was no way to go back. The life-giving bone marrow was gone.

The flame engulfed and began to burn me. You would think that it should eventually kill me and the torture would stop. But in Hell, we are already dead and this is what dead feels like. Dead is not a peace of any kind and it never ends. Dead is in Hell. God has separated death from Himself and put it in Hell.

The heat was unbearable, like nothing I have ever felt. My human skin dripped off my body because of the extreme heat. Wherever the flame burned me, the heat put an intense, tormenting pain in that place. It felt just like when I burned my hand cooking bacon. However, in Hell, instead of being able to soothe the burn with ice, my burns were wrapped in the heat of Hell. The pain was terrible and unthinkable.

My initial response to that heat was to protect myself, to curl up in a ball because the center of me hurt so much. I tried to protect the center of me because my spirit is there. As I curled up, the flame would hit me in different places to cause my body to snap out of this protective position because there is no form of relief in Hell. Hell is designed to torture endlessly. No one can close their eyes or go to sleep. There is no rest to be found. My inability to find relief caused my body to twist and contort in every unnatural way imaginable.

As far as I could see in every direction there were other flame cells with people being tortured. I could never get to them. They would never get to me. I was cast away from God. And all the time I kept regretting and wishing it was a minute ago.

These flames were not like a normal fire. They were alive and calculatingly wicked as they planned how they would attack. They burned like no other flame. I know of three fires. A fire on the earth, like a campfire, is burning because it has all the right ingredients. Take away an ingredient and it stops. The fire of Heaven never goes out because it is fueled with the knowledge and likeness of God. Our God is an all-consuming fire (see Jer. 4:4 AMP). However, the fire in Hell is evil. It burns as a remembrance of what it is like to disrespect, dishonor, and disobey the knowledge of God. It consumes everything that God has separated from Himself. He has separated sin as far as the east is from the west, and sin is in Hell being burned up forever. The fire there has the sole design and desire to torture, of course, because being without God is torture.

As the fire touched my body, it would cause me to uncurl from the tight ball that I was in so that the flames could find new spots to scorch and re-burn the areas already seared. It was even worse because I knew I could never heal from these burns. The flames made my body unrecognizable.

Hell is growing more wicked all the time in death. There is no life in Hell but death grows and has permeated everything of Hell. There is no earthly word for that. It was proud of its wickedness and in a sick way pleased that I knew just how wicked. This was incredibly and awfully frightening. God did not give us a spirit of fear (see 2 Tim. 1:7). The kind of fear in Hell is grown in darkness. Hell is filled with darkness and unspeakable, untranslatable fear. Inside the knowing is the knowledge that this darkness is never leaving and that it will take over *everything*. And the more time passed, the more the inky fog covered my cell blocking any hope of finding the gates that had brought me in. Hate became everything inside of the darkness. It was both a fuel and a by-product of the darkness. Time raced forward, and with each passing second Hell was more destruc-tive to me. Of course, because everything hurts when it's without God. Hopelessness!

CHAPTER 5

CHANGED FOREVER BY HELL

STRESS

Once, years ago, I lived next to a school. One day there was an alarming sound, and when I looked outside I realized there had been a terrible crash at the intersection in front of the school. Instinctively, I began running the short distance to the accident. There were two vehicles involved—a van and a car. The drivers both got out and the van driver opened the door to expose children in car seats. Without thinking, and all credit to the Holy Spirit, I jumped into the driver's seat of the car. Before I could process my surroundings, I reached out to push the passenger, a boy around 16 years old, into the side of the door. He was unconscious and his body was mangled in with the car door. He had a cut mark around his throat. I later learned that he had tried to commit suicide the day before by hanging himself. Because I did not know this, I thought somehow the accident had done that too. While trying to hold his head up and push his body against the side of the car door, I began screaming. When the people at the van heard me, they came over and said they would call for help. Many people came out of the school.

The boy was making gurgling noises. Even though I knew help was on the way, I couldn't stop yelling the word *help!* I knew supernaturally that as soon as he was free from the door his blood flow was going to explode. I knew this boy was dying.

Blood was everywhere, and that was terrifying for me. There was a kid about the same age in the back seat. A teacher from the school jumped in to evaluate him. He was bleeding from his head. His body was not mangled with the car but his seat belt was trapping him and he was also unconscious.

I heard the sirens and thought they were taking forever. I finally remembered to pray. I knew that for this kid to live, he needed a miracle from Jesus. The paramedics arrived and asked me to hold him up so that they could see if they could get him out of the front window. They could not. The Jaws of Life machine arrived. It wasn't working.

As I watched him, I felt death all around us. It freaked me out to feel that. The medical team decided to remove him from the driver's side. They covered the passenger window with a blanket to protect everyone inside and broke it so another person could reach in and hold the boy's body against the side of the door. The man in the backseat was replaced by a fireman who helped hold the boy in the front seat while I exited the car covered in blood.

The paramedic and several police officers pulled the teenager out and laid him on a stretcher. A policeman escorted me away from the immediate scene but still inside of the taped off area. I got on my knees right on top of broken glass and started praying that death would leave and the boy would live. I felt death until the ambulance left the scene. The policeman told me that I had played an important part. I thought he meant the prayer. He said that most people would not have thought to push someone into the door to stop the onslaught of bleeding. I explained that it was the Holy Spirit.

The policeman was a believer and he nodded. The boy lived, but the post-traumatic stress from that event was debilitating in my life. It took a long time for me to function normally again because I replayed the scene over and over in my mind.

That experience was nothing compared to the amount of stress I felt watching people suffer in Hell. Death is everywhere in Hell. It is hurting each person in serious ways. But Death is not that we die and everything stops. Death is the increase of pain and suffering forever with no hope of relief. There is no way to cry out to Jesus for help once we are in Hell. There is no spiritual wisdom to help save anyone else because the Holy Spirit does not dwell in Hell. And my brain kept replaying what I just saw perfectly because it was working at 100 percent capacity now. In Hell, there is no way to get the horrors my eyes took in out of my brain, so it could function the way it did before I saw it. There was a never-ending loop of horrendous thoughts, pictures, and agonies as I processed each new thing and my mind was filled with a hellish mental illness.

OVERWHELMED SENSES

Nothing works in unity in Hell.

I tried to shut my eyes because I was so afraid. I had never been that afraid. I scrunched my face to lock my eyelids and rest my eyes, but there is no form of rest or relief in Hell. The air there burned my eyes, but no tears would come to moisten them. Somehow the flame forced my eyes open and sealed them that way. In the process they broke apart so that they would not work together. Sealed eternally open to constantly dart back and forth in great pain and fear. My eyes were frantically looking, watching. *What can I see? Where am I?* They would never close again.

When I was a child, I was in the room when a relative was in excruciating pain with their eyes open. Their eyes darted wildly back and forth. Eventually they passed out, which was a relief for everyone. I knew that this was what my eyes were doing. The feelings of vertigo were just the beginning. I couldn't process what I was seeing. Our eyes either have to work together to process images correctly or one has to be covered or shut off. Two eyes seeing two different things sends conflicting messages into the brain. My brain was unable to handle the conflict of images. It caused me to continuously dry heave.

My eyes did not want to see the blackness, the fear, and other flames with people trapped in them. I could barely see inside the other flames but what I saw was people being tortured, flames flying across the spans of Hell from cell to cell, transforming people out of the image of God. It is a different kind of trauma to be incapable of helping. It is very painful, stressful, and sickening to watch other people in pain.

I saw the space of Hell moving and expanding as time was almost completed. There was so much blackness. If the flame was not directly in front of me then I could see the people trapped in other flames. But when the flame was over my face, everything was utter blackness. To clarify, the flame in Hell is not colorful. It's not red, yellow, orange, blue, or white. The flames filling Hell are darkness. Like the color black, but not quite. Black is a good color because God has made wonderful things that are black like the onyx stone, the color of my little dog, and the strong thick hair of Asian people.

Inside of Heaven and Hell there are things that we don't have the language to describe. There is no color to explain darkness. Darkness is not a color. It is an oppressive evil devoid of any kind of light. Black is a descriptive word to explain the color of dark things in the same way we often use white to explain the color of light. However, black and darkness have the same relatable issue as the ocean problem. I can only attempt to describe darkness with the word *black*, but it doesn't even scratch the surface. They are really nothing alike. Darkness is so much worse. When the Lord talks about darkness, He isn't talking about the color black. We say Jesus is a bright white light and I have seen that light, but it isn't white like we know white. In Heaven light filled me; in Hell, darkness consumed me.

All around me was dreadfully dark. Not dark like what we have outside at nighttime. This darkness just kept (and keeps) growing as it created ever-increasing fear. It moved like a sneaky, deceptive fog. If you have ever watched a scary movie, you know the way they use the music so that you know something bad is about to happen. This is what that darkness was somehow able to do. It had a sound to it. One that shot fear into every thought and caused my body to further contort.

While I was watching, unable to shut my eyes, the evil flame licked around looking for ways to burn me that would cause the most pain. I wished I could hold still and that the flame leave me alone. The contorting it caused was extremely painful, and I moved in ways that I was not designed to move. Have you ever seen someone being beaten with a belt? Their body contorts to the movement of the belt. Instinctively, the body moves in a way to get that hurt part away from the belt. I am sure that this is what my body did there. It was like a beating with a flame instead of a belt.

I thought if I could hold still for just a minute I might find some relief. I have back problems. I have been in several serious car accidents, had a spinal tap go very wrong, and have broken my tailbone. I understand back pain. I'll describe it as white pain. When you throw your back out, it seems like everything hurts. You tighten your eyes and a cold sweat comes over you and you don't want to move as if your nerves are on fire. When it happens I don't want anyone to touch me or move me. I'm in so much pain and the only thing I can think about is the pain.

I had that feeling in Hell but it was magnified many times over. In the violent contorting of my body, I broke my own back and dislocated my limbs. All of these painful moves transformed my body into conformity with Hell itself. I was becoming a hellish creature. Everything was hurting at the same time. My mind, will, emotions, physical body, and spirit hurt all at the same time. Though I longed to be still for a minute, that was never going to happen.

New regret was added to the heaping measure I already owned. Again, words fail to convey the fullness of this experience. The longer I was there, the stronger the flames and the contorting became until every bone was disjointed, every tendon was torn, and every nerve was ripped apart. My body short-circuited and was becoming a fixture of Hell, forever changed, forged in the heat, pain, and flame of Hell.

In Hell, any opening in my body was bad because somehow it is forced and sealed open. For example, the sounds of Hell are excruciating. I wanted to cover up my ears with my hands to stop the amount of noise coming into my brain but I couldn't. That opening was forever opened and the sound of Hell was the sound of fear. And how do I explain that? It's like the ocean problem again. The sound was so hurtful that all I could do was shake my head in hopes of moving so quickly that the noise couldn't enter.

There were other people in Hell and they were making noise with their bodies. I heard bones cracking and breaking along with the vocal noises in utter agony. I was making the same kind of noise with my body and vocal cords. Horrific sounds of torment assaulted my ears. Today if I were to hear any of those sounds again, I am positive I would begin to wail. I wish I could have cried in Hell, but there are no tears there because my body was absent of all water.

I heard one time the sound of a mother who had just gotten news that her baby had died. I was in an emergency room waiting for a friend when I heard her. Even today, the remembrance of that noise is unsettling. There is a sound when something hurts that deeply. It comes out of the depths of the being. When this woman's agony came out, it didn't start out small but went off suddenly like an emergency alarm. I had no idea what had happened, but I knew something was terribly wrong and I jumped to my feet and rushed out of my friend's cubicle to run and help. As I was moving, my body responded with deep emotion because of the sound she was making. My eyes leaked an abundance of tears and my heart was filled with mercy and compassion. I would have done anything for that momma.

They medicated her. But while she was screaming it was as if she was a tuning fork and she had tuned me into a raw pain that was hidden somewhere in my core. This is the noise of weeping and wailing that the Bible speaks of in Hell (see Matt. 8:12; 13:42). And all of us suffering in Hell were tuning forks for each other. We each tuned in and felt, to the core of our being, the height and depth of the pain of every other person there.

When I was in Hell, the screams of others were deafening. Every single voice of pain stood out individually. We were each a tuning fork for the next person and it was horrible. Hell is not a quiet place; in fact, I think it is the noisiest place I've ever been. It was so loud that my ear drums burst. These sounds and the volume of noise in Hell caused such an unbearable panic inside of me.

I felt no mercy or compassion, because those things are not in Hell. Instead, I felt hatred toward the others who were also suffering and screaming in agony because it was partially their fault that I was in such pain. There was no room in me for compassion or mercy. Those are attributes of God and nothing of His nature is there. My hatred quickly grew to self-hatred, which is huge in Hell.

I have very sensitive ears. As a child we had chalkboards and when someone scratched one it made a sound that short-circuited me. I discovered back then that I could relieve the pain of that sound by yelling. This principle was true in Hell as well. I was yelling to try and take some of the pressure off my ears. However, like on the earth when we yell, it caused a lot of stress in my whole body and used up large amounts of energy.

There are no words in Hell. We didn't need to say words because all the words had been used. There were only sounds of agony.

Sometimes when I am preaching the Word of God, there comes an anointing. When it comes, knowledge, understanding, revelation, and clarity flow into my mind rapidly and constantly. In Hell, I had a similar flow, which gave me the ability to process everything about Hell, every bad thing about my life, and how righteous it was that I and the other people around me were in Hell.

My thoughts were going faster than my thoughts here can go. My mind was on super warp speed. When I first arrived in Hell there was some comfort in knowing that I was remembered by other people on the earth. Yet as the minutes ticked by and the flames burned and Hell intensified, the knowledge that I was being forgotten became overwhelming. You see, we were never designed to be forgotten.

To know that people were forgetting me heaped more pain. I knew they were going to Heaven and Jesus was going to wipe away their tears about me and they would forget me (see Ps. 34:15-16). I hated this so much. It caused more hate to grow inside of my heart about all the people whom I loved on the earth who were not in Hell. Then I started comparing. I knew bad things they had done, and I wanted them in Hell too.

I just can't even believe this was me. Today, I wouldn't want my worst enemy to go to Hell, but while I was there I wanted past friends and enemies to also suffer. The darkness in my heart had no constraints and was allowed to become exceedingly wicked.

The knowledge that this was going to last forever was overwhelming. And, even worse, everything kept speeding up. The twisting, turning, and burning was moving so fast that I knew I would be like Satan in no time at all—an utter enemy of God, hating Him too.

CHANGED ETERNALLY ON THE INSIDE

It was so hot in Hell. I tried to breathe, but I couldn't. I could only gasp because the air was too hot and noxious. When I breathed it in, it burned, poisoned, and crippled me.

It reminded me of a when I was up on a mountain at 14,000 feet above sea level and found out that I couldn't breathe. I could take in the air but my lungs couldn't process it. I was overcome by a strange feeling that quickly became a scary one. The group I was with purchased an air tank to help, but the only way to truly fix the problem was to get me off that mountain. I just simply could not catch my breath. So it was in Hell.

Another time, I was swimming at my grandparents' house. They had a lake nearby with a boat in the water that I tried to climb into from the side. I didn't have enough upper body strength to pull myself up into the boat. So, I wrapped my feet around a rope to climb over the boat's edge. Instead, I fell into the water and the rope caused me to hang upside down with my face underwater where I couldn't breathe. I remember kicking and trying to scream, which made the whole thing worse. Someone saw my problem and jumped in to pick me up. There was no way to breath underwater; the only hope was to get me out of the lake. So it was in Hell.

Not being able to breathe is bad. The type of air in Hell hurt so much that when I took it in, it brought more death and fear and placed them firmly on the inside of me. I knew with the first gulp that I took, *"This is very bad."* But I couldn't get away. In my panic all I could do was try to take a deeper breath. I only took one deep breath. It was enough to know to never do it again. The air there is designed to bring more pain, more fear, and more torture. There is no breath of life in Hell!

Because the air hurts, I tried to only take as much as I needed. There was never any relief. I tried to breathe through my nose but the stench made me instantly sick. Everything reeked of a smell I have never experienced. Take every bad smell you can imagine—sulfur, ammonia mixed with bleach, toxic chemicals, and maybe that might come close.

I was incredibly sick, nauseated, and had a tremendous headache. I just wanted to lie down. I wanted to remember the times when Mike would come in and ask me, "Do you want a cool rag?" He'd get me medicine and bring me something to drink. I longed for somebody to take care of me. As soon as those thoughts came, they were whisked away. They were good thoughts, and that is a measure of relief not allowed in Hell.

The more I breathed in the toxic air, the more my body changed. It transformed my human body, the image of God, into a body fit for Hell. This whole process was constant agony and constant pain that was never going to stop.

CHAPTER 6

UNIMAGINABLE HELL

UNIMAGINABLE HELL

Hell is truly unimaginable, but I want to make sure that I give you some dimensions and facts about it. There is no water in Hell. The torment and the heat and the fire have increased since the day the Lord created it and removed it from Himself. If there was a drop of water, it might be able to put out one of those wicked flames. But there is not even one drop.

Hell is big and was expanding while I was there to accommodate the numbers of people getting ready to arrive. It is made from darkness and there are levels of darkness that at first cannot be seen. But as the eyes adjust, the deeper levels of darkness are seen and experienced. Each being in Hell actually becomes the darkness.

As a child, I got a bad cold and woke up with my eyes stuck shut with gunk. I instantly panicked. I tried very hard to separate my eyelids and actually hurt them in my panic. I remember not being able to see and wondering if this was what it was like to be blind. I have to tell you, not being able to see on earth is nothing like in Hell. There is no comparison between the darkness of Hell and either closing our eyes or being in a room with the lights off making it difficult to see. Again it's like trying to explain the ocean with a glass of water.

The atmosphere in Hell is completely evil and becoming more so. There is no joy. In fact, what we call depression on the earth would be considered joyful in Hell.

In my past I fought depression. It lasted so long that eventually, I was suicidal. I remember the devastation and how alone I felt in it. The worst depression is *nothing* in comparison to the heart-sickness that I felt in Hell. The Bible says that hope deferred makes the heart sick (see Prov. 13:12). When a heart is sick, it is death. Death really is separation from God. It is hopelessness, darkness, a living sickness.

As I've said before, time in Hell was speeding up to reach a climatic point. I knew that the time wasn't yet as many people were continually entering Hell because of their personal rejection of Jesus.

Hell is sealed by the big gates that I saw when my vision began and I entered Hell. Before I was dragged through the gates, I could see them, but inside Hell I could not. They were sealed in flames on the inside.

An aspect of the final judgment will be when Hell is cast into the lake of fire (see Rev. 20:14). That had not happened yet and is still to come.

Hell was very big in that it encompassed a large geographical area, and at that time there were so many people there. I knew Hell grew to hold all those coming to spend eternity there (see Isa. 5:14). I also understood that more people were in Hell than in Heaven (see Matt. 7:14). This thought makes me cry. How many people were in Hell? Not one of them was made to live in that awful place. It was 100 percent righteous for them to be there, but each of them could have chosen Jesus.

While there, I was in a section reserved for my family. I knew that I had relatives there. I've grappled to handle this. I know that I am a son of Adam, a daughter of Eve, and therefore everybody in Hell is my relative. But I felt that I was surrounded by people who knew me. They were ones who on the earth I would have called my family. I hated them. And I hated that my ancestors had not had a stronger relationship with Jesus to point my family, and eventually me, in the right direction.

I can remember as a child when a family member received something I wanted. It broke and I was happy because I didn't want them to have it. That's how I felt toward everyone around me, even those I knew to be my own family. I was filled with this sick, gleeful, twisted hatred that they were also in pain. It hurts me to share these terrible things about the wickedness that was me.

Many of the people in Hell are ones who did not love God on the earth, but there were also people there like me—Christians. They knew Jesus was who He said He was and they believed He meant what He said, but they didn't believe it enough to change. They were just like me—unforgiving.

There is nothing we can do for anyone in Hell. If someone is there, it's too late. Can God change His mind? Yes, God can do whatever He desires. Just as God was able to put me in Hell and take me out of Hell, He can do anything He chooses. Please understand that God is a good Father and He allows us to choose. People choose Hell. My family had chosen unbelief in Jesus and had also chosen Hell. I hated that they had not walked with Jesus. But I was not there because of their sin; I was there because of my own. No one gets to say, "Because of my family, I didn't know I was supposed to serve God."

FOREVER CHANGED

One of the terrifying things that happened while I was in Hell came from something like demonic beings who were on the move. They were tiny little dark things. I call them black holes because they absorbed the darkness into supreme darkness. They were in complete opposition to God, filled with nothing but hatred toward Him. They were allowed to pass through me.

That little section they passed through was immediately and eternally changed. Just as my heart had been hardened, that piece became hate—forever set against God. The black holes made it so that all partnership with God was dissolved. I was cut off from any notion of peace, eternally. Each time that blackness passed through me, I would scream with agony.

When we were saved, Jesus replaced our heart of stone with a heart of flesh (see Ezek. 36:26). It is just the opposite in Hell. The heart turns to a heart of—not even stone, but of evil. The heart of a person in Hell is to utterly despise everyone and be utterly despised.

No Relief

In Hell, there is no sleep, no slumber, and it is impossible to find rest. The Bible says, "*They have no rest day or night, who worship the beast and his image*," and "*I will both lie down in peace, and sleep; for You alone, O Lord, make me dwell in safety*" (Rev. 14:11; Ps. 4:8). Everything in Hell is overwhelming and desperate. When bad things happen to me on earth, they are exhausting and I find strength and rejuvenation in just taking a nap. Or I would end a bad day by believing that things would be better when I woke up after a refreshing night of sleep. In Hell, my mind was never allowed to shut off, to rest from the agony, or to have a refreshing dream.

Also, there is no self-control in Hell. Everyone is being controlled as they are filled with more and more hatred. I didn't want to touch anybody, and I knew no one was ever going to touch me again. Even if I could have gone to another person, I was so filled with hatred that all I would have done was hurt them. I can only compare it to some of the evil acts that are currently done on the earth. How people hurt others and do terrible things to them. We think it is horrible, but in Hell that's all anyone wants to do—hurt others.

When I was depressed on the earth, I hated to be by myself because I was tempted by a real enemy, self-hatred. I constantly fought that self-loathing. In Hell, self-hatred is magnified a million times. Because nothing good exists in Hell, there are no good words to combat that enemy. The Bible says, *"You shall love your neighbor as yourself"* (Mark 12:31). In Hell, you hate one another as you hate yourself.

Hell is 100 percent perverted. There is no decency or humanity there, no humanitarian acts. Everyone is beastly—far more revolting than any earthly beast. Everyone becomes evil. Hell and its inhabitants are evil. I experienced being evil. I felt the evil and I have waged war against those places in my heart that, here on the earth, have even a semblance of that evil.

WEIGHT OF SIN

One of the things I experienced in Hell was the guilt accumulated during my life on the earth and the fruit that guilt had produced. I was accused, found guilty, and then sentenced. I was only in Hell long enough to process three accusations—unkindness, harshness, and impatience.

Now I want to explain, as best I can, what I understood in Hell. On the day that I was saved, I went to Jesus and I repented, turned from my wicked ways, and allowed Jesus to cover that sin. I was made clean. So all of the sins that I had done up until the year 2000, when I came to know Jesus, were separated from me. Where were they separated to? Well, sin goes to Hell, separated from God in a place where He remembers no more. God is not in Hell, so He's not remembering all the sin that is there.

Hell is the keeper of sin. Sin does not stop growing there. In fact, it grows at a faster rate as the environment is favorable for its growth. My sins were in Hell; they had my name and actions tied to them. As the Divine sentencing was revealed, they entered back into me, into every cell of my being (see Matt. 18:32-35).

I began expanding in a grotesque way. I was becoming the sins I had committed. I don't even know how to explain it—like growths, tumors, sickness, and swollenness all over me.

In Hell, I realized that sin is alive, like a cancer in our bodies. The only way to rid ourselves of it is to forgive. That is available on the earth while living, but it is not available to the lost souls who have died and are in Hell where it is too late.

The Bible says that the joy of the Lord is my strength. One keeps getting stronger and growing in joy. Similarly, in Hell sin continues to grow and strengthen in destruction, despair, disease, dysfunction, and every bad thing.

Each sentence handed down to me had two parts. The first was how that sin had been done to me and the second was how I had committed that sin. It shocked me, the amount and weight of how many unkind things had been done to me over the course of my lifetime. Even things I had forgotten were all stacked in piles around me. Each unkind sin had produced a memory marker in me. I had used it to grow it into what I thought was knowledge or wisdom to protect myself. But we can never protect ourselves with a weapon of the enemy! I had coddled those sins and let them shape me in how I treated other people and how open, or closed, I was to others, even people I loved.

However, the amount or weight of the sin done against me was never more than I had committed myself. The stacks of sins that had wounded me were *nothing* compared to the stacks and stacks of sins that I had done in hurting other people.

Many people have terrible pasts with unthinkable hurts. Mine is not squeaky clean. I could see how the sinful things done to me shaped parts of my life. But just the opposite should have happened. I knew what it felt like to be hurt and sinned against. I should never have hurt anyone else. Yet, because I had not forgiven those people and I had hung on to the memories of those hurts, the sin of not forgiving each person fully controlled me when I was sentenced in Hell (see James 1:14-27). If I had only forgiven the people who had sinned against me, those sins would have never been in Hell waiting for me because I would not have been in Hell (see Matt. 6:15).

Unkindness

The first accusation against me was, "You are not kind." I was forced to process the stacks of sins pertaining to my unkindness. As a daughter, there were many unkind acts toward my parents stacked there. As a sister, I had more stacks of unkind acts against my siblings. I was chosen to be the oldest by God, but I had tried to find ways to not have my younger siblings around me. As a wife, I have been unkind to my husband. As a mother, friend, coworker, neighbor, driver, passenger, etc. You get the picture. All of these unkind deeds, thoughts, and words showed up as evidence that I belonged in Hell.

Harshness

The next accusation was, "You are not gentle." I processed all of the times when I was pushed, pulled, beaten up, and spoken to harshly. The stack was of good size, but there is no comparison to how big the stack was of all the ungentle things I had done to others. Grabbing someone and hurting them. How I had stuffed a crying daughter into her car seat or held her down so that I could change a diaper. Trust me the list goes on and on. And I knew exactly what I was doing at the time. I thought it was them that had made me this way. Instead, it was me. It was unforgiveness that had made me this way. Things were done to me that were very harsh. But knowing firsthand what that felt like, I should have never been harsh to others. Instead, I had chosen to be less and less gentle.

Every sin began at my age of accountability. Imagine that you have a tally sheet where everything is kept to give you an accurate score. You start racking up points and even double scoring. With one sin you are both not kind and not gentle, so that sin is counted in both areas. In Hell, I saw that I was a monster! If I had been judged only on being unkind, the sentence of Hell was righteous. I was grotesque in my own thinking. In looking at the stacks of sins, I knew I was the chief sinner. I was the meanest, most hateful, deplorable person I had ever met.

Impatience

The third sentence was, "You are not patient!" Again, first were the times that people had been impatient with me and what that produced in my life. We do affect one another. All the impatience I had learned from leaders and family members around me taught me to not be patient and I saw how that had wounded and shaped me.

This truth brought me so much pain. I faintly remembered my first trip to Heaven. I had been taught by the Lord Himself, the long-suffering Lord Jesus who loves me so. In Heaven, Jesus had been so patient with me! He presented Himself to me in a world of patience. His patience healed so much of my heart. I believe it was His patience that convinced me to trust Him and ultimately to give Him my life. His attribute to be so longsuffering is simply stunning (see 2 Pet. 3:9). People treat Him, *I treated Him*, badly for many years. And yet He responds with patience. He is the truest example of patience. I had no excuse. I was taught by the best. As these grotesque facts of my impatience were brought back to me, I could not handle my own wealth of cruelty.

Hell was the most impatient place. It wouldn't stop hurrying and hurting. I crossed from regret into despair. There is no despair like the despair of Hell. The despair was fed by the knowledge of how utterly despicable and evil I was. The most unthinkable hurt was to know how true and good and right it was for me to be in Hell burning and twisting. I agreed with God's judgment and I realized I was not His anymore.

There were other judgments that I was going to have to process that were attached to other sins I had committed. I knew they were opposite of the fruits of the Spirit. I knew I was not loving, joyful, peaceful, patient, kind, good, gentle, faithful, or self-controlled.

Sin is evil! Sin has a weight and hurts now and it hurts there. The Bible tells us to abstain from every sort of evil (see 1 Thess. 5:22). We are to flee from sin. Flee from the devil. Flee from his ways. But I thought I could handle it. You know all those little pet sins? All those ones that we tell ourselves that someday we'll get over? I had no idea before going to Hell how much sin God saved me from. In Hell, the sins of my earthly life just kept coming. Stacks of sins of things that I didn't even know I had done. I did not fully process all of those while I was in Hell. That's how much sin I had in my life. That was a glimpse of how much evil I had allowed in my life on earth and how much Jesus had forgiven me.

Again, I thought, *why hadn't I forgiven those people?* I wouldn't have been there and all of the stacks of sins could not have come back to me if I had just forgiven people (see Matt. 18:31-35).

All that sin, it was waiting for me. It was mine, and it was going to have me. It wracked my whole being with sickness. I watched my body become a cancerous, disgusting, hurtful thing and yet knew it could have all been avoided through obedience to Jesus.

The darkness—I was the darkness. I hated God, although I understood that He was righteous and good, and the separation was right. Hell is a righteous judgement of God, and I knew my being there was righteous. What was unimaginable had become my reality forever.

CHAPTER 7

GOD'S GARMENT

The most devastating thing that happened to me in Hell was at the very beginning. It was God rending His garment. His mighty right hand reached up and He tore His judgment robe, with all the power that was in Him. It ripped across His heart and the symbolism and rendering of the prophetic act undid me. Above all, this was the deepest and most violent pain that happened. And even though everything else was a new pain, nothing compared to this pain. *Nothing!* It began the releasing of Hell in my life. I understood the supernatural significance of the rending—that it was so much worse than any separation we can imagine on earth. God was done with me! I was dead to God!

How to explain this pain? I have things in my family line that are wrong. One of the things that my ancestors have passed down through the ages is turning from the family and cutting out family members. In my genealogy, someone decided he was going to leave the family so he changed his last name and began his own family line. He lived in the same area as his relatives but they never spoke. Grandparents never knew their grandbabies, family celebrations were never complete, and a very demonic principle was introduced into our bloodlines.

It has happened in my lifetime as well. All of a sudden, this cousin is out of our family over the price of a car. That aunt is no longer a part of us because of where she chooses to live. This sister is no longer a part of the family because of how she grieved the loss of her mother. That uncle's funeral is done immediately and in secret to stop certain relatives from attending and in the process preventing everyone from attending. I have seen this same evil in friendships, working relationships, even inside the Church.

I know the pain personally. I too have been cut out. Marked as an outcast. Abandoned, beaten down, and thrown away as if I was worthless. It is a deep hurt to be an outcast, the black sheep. If I dwell on it for any length of time, it becomes crippling. The traffic it creates in my mind, will, and emotions, not to mention the stress in my physical body creates a deep depression. Everyone playing God and handing out judgments on His behalf to leave people out. This is very different from people openly choosing despicable things.

I am not innocent of the behavior. Before I was saved, I participated in the practice myself, believing that the person cut off was getting what they deserved. And in some twisted way of manipulation, believing that my mistreatment would in some way help them. What a lie!

Being cut off by God, however, is in a category all its own. We are His creation. Made for the purpose of being close to Him and each other. Sin is what separates us from God and from each other.

When God ripped His garment, it meant that I was no longer a part of Him. When it is final for God, it is final. He is a judge, and His judgments are always righteous and final. If I had received the gifts of mercy and grace, I would have fared better in being able to forgive. I did not understand the power of the cross.

There are many people in Hell. Too many people! We can't do anything about that. But how many of our family are going there? You know what? Most of us really don't care. The Bible says Hell is getting bigger to hold all the people who are coming (see Isa. 5:14; Deut. 32:22). We should be doing something about it.

> *Dear friends, let us love one another, for love comes from God. Everyone who loves has been born of God and knows God. Whoever does not love does not know God, because God is love* (1 John 4:7-8 NIV).

> *Keep yourselves in the love of God looking for the mercy of our Lord Jesus Christ unto eternal life. And on some have compassion, making a distinction; but others save with fear, pulling them out of the fire, hating even the garment defiled by the flesh* (Jude 1:21-23).

It was the mercy of Jesus that He sent me to Hell and His mercy that He took me out of there. It was His kindness. It was His gentleness. It was just like when He saved me. But I didn't know that. I didn't know the day Jesus saved me that He saved me from all of Hell's torments. I didn't know when I celebrated freedom that He saved me from the bondage to sin and Hell's eternal punishments.

It hurts to tell you this. It hurts to tell you about the punishment that was mine. It was Jesus' mercy and love that picked me up and brought me back from Hell. If I had died in that vision, I would still be there.

CHAPTER 8

THE AFTERMATH

NEVER THE SAME AGAIN

I reentered the earthly realm yelling. The worship was still going on, but I took center stage from the back of the room with my screaming.

I had no idea how much trouble I was in or that I would be forever changed. I had no grid for the loss or the gain that would surround my life from that day forward. Today, I still have an eerie weightiness whenever I share about Hell. It is a very important topic that everyone should take seriously.

My boss quickly walked back to where I stood. He put his hands on my shoulders to get my attention. But I could not place his face or how I knew him. I was utterly undone. The brightness of the room was the first direct contrast I recognized. I shut my eyes against that burning brightness that stunned me after the darkness of Hell.

I found I could actually shut my eyes. I would not open them because I felt overwhelming shame. My brain was in so much pain and shock, but somehow I knew I was not in Hell anymore. But I wasn't sure where I was standing.

An incredible gratitude flooded me as I realized that I was not burning or twisting. However, I was in a whirling, mindless panic that the nightmare would return.

As I finally opened my eyes, I saw a person. I grabbed ahold of him. I knew that I needed people and I did not want to be alone anymore. This was in direct opposition to the person I was before I went to Hell. Before, I didn't want people to touch me and I didn't need to touch people. People hurt people, so I kept them at a distance.

My boss was trying to get me to answer the question, "What is wrong?" I could not understand the question. *Everything* was wrong!

I could sense a demon in the room threatening me not to tell anyone where I had been or else. It kept reminding me of how much of a monster I was. I thought the "or else" was that I would go back to Hell. The demon was right. I was a monster. If any of us could see the weight of sin we carried before Jesus delivered us, we would all agree we are monsters.

Something about my boss seemed distantly familiar. Maybe it was his voice or his authority, but there was something that caused my mind to try to connect with him. Familiarity—with it there was a small level of security that entered me. He was familiar and a good memory came to the forefront of my mind. More security came when I felt his concern for me. It was life-giving to feel genuine concern.

Concern somehow brings *hope*. Knowing that I was not alone brought hope rising up in me. I think that if hope had not entered in at that moment, I would have died. The Bible says that hope deferred makes the heart sick (see Prov. 13:12). I agree. I had no hope in Hell, and the result was death.

My boss' smile was a coaxing gift that allowed me to venture a look into his eyes. Human eyes are very powerful. I have heard that they are the windows to the soul. The Bible says that our eyes are the lamps to the body, and if our eyes are clear then our whole body will be full of light (see Matt.

6:22). By reason, the opposite is true. If our eyes are darkened in sin, then our whole body will be filled with darkness.

I had never really noticed the light in his eyes, or the amount of brotherly love toward me. I needed that. We all *need* it from each other. The kindness seemed so foreign, and I clung to it as a way to stay connected to this reality.

But the trauma was too much to hold inside.

My senses were on a negative overload. Everything hurt, including my eyes, ears, mouth, body, memories, identity, and my assurance of salvation. I hurt. At the same time, the love in the room was a new overload to my overburdened circuits. To feel so much love for each other and Jesus in a room was something that I had only felt on a few previous occasions. But on August 28th, the room was filled with love. It was filled with love for me. This knowledge would help me in the years to come as I processed this experience.

My eyes burned from *fear*. All I could see was fear. My eyes were darting around trying to get my bearings. They hurt from the images I had seen in Hell. It was as if I had woken from the worst nightmare ever but I could not fully wake up. I realized that the excruciating pain of my eyes being broken apart was now gone and I could shut them. So I did. Then I quickly opened them because fear of going back would not let me keep my eyes shut.

I felt like my life was that of a pendulum. It had swung so quickly that I was still experiencing two realities.

My voice was raw. I instinctively knew that I needed to stop yelling as that act was hurting and stressing my entire being. The ability to be silent was a direct contrast from the intensity and hopelessness of screaming in Hell. I could not have stopped making noise there because silence cannot exist in Hell.

Supernatural Help

The noise I was making was now more of a whimper compared to what it had been. I noticed right away an immediate difference in the pronunciation of sounds. I had a tongue on earth; I did not have a tongue in Hell. About that time, I realized an angel was beside me. He told me that the wickedest part of a person is their tongue and that mine did not go to Hell. I accepted this right away as I recalled not having a tongue there. This fact would later be a cornerstone in my fight to regain my life on earth and understand that my experience was only a vision. I hung on to the fact that if the wickedest part of my body, my tongue, was not in Hell, there was still hope for me. It helped me believe the vision was not just to tell me I would go to Hell when I died, which helped me seek out and reach for God.

In all fairness, I have no idea how long the angel had been with me, but I do believe that the knowledge of my tongue was given by the one standing next to me whom I couldn't see. The angel was telling me that I am greatly loved. At the time, I did not know to whom the angel was speaking. You can imagine that I was freaked out by anything supernatural. I did not welcome the angel, ask questions, or understand. I was traumatized.

I have spent years recalling every detail. I believe that the angel was there bringing in the things I needed to live and to move forward one step at a time. The reality about my tongue immediately brought me comfort. I know that in my state of mind, I would have never thought about my tongue on my own.

My mind, during those first moments back, was still working at the supernatural full capacity. Although my mind's capabilities did not stay at that level long, even a moment of that ability on the earth was another absolute overload. It was like I lived a whole lifetime in a minute. Definitely overwhelming and back to a huge ocean problem to try and explain.

In that short time that my mind was working at full capacity, I kept thinking, "Oh my God, I am going back to Hell!" I was able to say this to my boss. Fortunately, he knew other people who had been to Hell and he had others in the room begin to pray for me. He also had a woman nearby hold me. I sobbed into her hair and held on to her as if my life depended on it. I wanted everyone to help me stop Hell from getting me again.

Though my boss did not know even a small portion of what I had experienced, he called for my husband to come and get me.

I was exhausted. No, that is not right. There is no expression to explain the state I was in. I was beyond exhausted—depleted, emptied, abandoned, hurt, mortified, wounded, terrified, and rejected. *Rejected*, by far, was the worst.

The woman who was holding me sat down on the floor and I cradled as much as I could of myself into her lap, especially my head. I could not feel God in my body, but I could feel Him in hers and my head needed to be covered in the love of Christ. I knew that the Bible says that people perish because of a lack of knowledge (see Hos. 4:6). I somehow knew that I needed my mind protected. The woman would shush me to try to get me to rest, but I was too upset. I knew there was going to be a battle over my mind. I felt the unseen one standing next to me was somehow also covering my mind against the tremendous attack.

I couldn't stop shaking. My body was in shock. I was thirstier than I have ever been. I drank two bottles of water but I still felt extremely parched.

I listened to the heart of the one I couldn't see and the lullaby singing of the woman holding me. I tried to rest or shut off. Neither happened.

Normal memories began returning, fragments of good times, but I couldn't shake the horrific Hell memory. I could not leave it behind. The pain and reality of Hell was too much and, of course, knowing that the unforgiveness was still inside of me was more terrible. It was all an overwhelming, life-changing reality. I couldn't snap out of it. Hell had marked me and I was afraid that it was going to search for me and suck me out of a room again.

I started trying to cut off the ropes that attached me to Hell. I could feel them as if they were wrapped around me. At the time I explained it as if I were a hot air balloon and the ties, instead of holding me to the ground, were holding me to Hell.

With every part of my being, I wanted out of the room where the gates to Hell had opened. But my frame felt too weak to move. I was afraid to look at the front of the room. I thought I was safer on the floor. I was positive I could describe those gates in detail. Today, I am thankful that I cannot. I knew I had gone to Hell because of unforgiveness and I was positive that I would return immediately. I did not know *how* to forgive. I was afraid to talk to God.

PARALYZING FEAR

I was *afraid* to talk to God. I brought this fear back with me from Hell and the realization of this excited the demon. I can't begin to tell you what kind of fear that breeds. If we cannot talk to the only One who can chase away darkness, then who can we talk too? I was afraid to bring any attention to myself at all. I knew that God had ripped His garments against me. I didn't want Him to know that somehow I escaped Hell. My only hope was to forgive everyone somehow and then when He found out, He might have mercy on me. *Crazy* right? It was a crazy and terrifying time.

The woman who held me prayed in tongues over me while we were waiting for my husband to arrive. I am sure that this idea was directed by the angel beside us. For a time I could hear them both praying. It was the best possible thing anyone could have done for me. I believe that through her prayers she made the demon leave and provided much needed stability to a volatile situation. I was unable to do anything of spiritual significance for myself. Today, I am so thankful to her and the angel who assisted me.

When Mike arrived, I did not recognize him either. As he bent down I knew that this man was upset. I didn't want to talk with him, let alone go with him. Mike had left an important meeting to come get me, but no one would tell him why I needed him to come quickly. He wanted an explanation and when I couldn't/wouldn't talk, he grew angrier. He had no grid for what had happened to me or for what we were going to face up ahead. I had gone to Heaven on different occasions, which always filled me with a great love, never panic and isolation. The whole thing blindsided him.

I probably could not have spoken anything intelligent, but the reason I wouldn't speak is that I recognized something in me toward Mike and I knew that he was a person I needed to forgive. I realized that I needed to forgive Mike before I realized he was my husband. I wasn't sure where to start. I was afraid of the unforgiveness that I could feel so clearly now. I was afraid that it would open up the door to Hell again and suck me in.

Can I share something with you? I still feel this today. I believe that unforgiveness is so serious that it could take me back to Hell. I don't mess with it. You know when someone hurts you how you try to do the mind thing and convince yourself that it is no big deal? You do all the mental gymnastics to quickly build a wall that removes you from that person and their life? Don't do it. It is a really big deal! *Feel* it inside. Once you can feel it, you can deal with it. I think too many people reject feelings as if they are not real. And sometimes at church we are taught that we cannot trust feelings because they are fickle. A human heart *feels* and it can feel unforgiveness. Deal with it because the consequence of unforgiveness is Hell. I know people don't like for me to say it this way. God forgave and so must we...or else.

WHERE TO EVEN BEGIN?

Mike put me in our car to take me home. I still couldn't speak. Anger in general is not good and it is rare for any anger to be considered righteous. Mike was angry and it was not righteous. Anger fuels unforgiveness and is like the fog that was in my Hell cell. It hides the way out. It clouds everything we feel. Anger is like a fire on earth but we can stop it. It has elements and if we take one away, we end the destruction that demolishes love. Anger if left alone turns to hate. I have found that to stop it I must *love* greater. I must be vulnerable, transparent, and willing. Some might call it weak, but I believe it is powerful to be that open in the face of anger. Just like when I entered Hell I left the positive past behind and engulfed hate. Anger does that too. It leaves out the positive past and engulfs us in more and more anger in hopes of it turning into hate.

When Mike got me home, we were in an emotional separation. God has linked us with certain people in an emotional dependence (see Rom. 12:4-5; 2 Tim. 2:24-25; 1 Pet. 4:10-11). Being separated from them is an emergency and can cause death. There are people God chooses for us whom we can trust. They are not perfect, but they are people we can wrestle with so we may continue in an emotional dependency with them. Everyone needs others! Mike is one of those emotional ties for me. He is a person I need to live with in emotional connection. Mike loves me and is my protector. He knows me better than anyone. For most of us, there are only a few dear people who know us that way. It makes them all the more invaluable.

I believe now that this separation was a ploy of the enemy. It was meant to isolate me, end my marriage, and destroy any chance of the forgiveness that needed to take place. The angel was still nearby and I believe he somehow helped calm Mike so he could pray for me. I kept telling Mike that I was going to have to go back to Hell. The panic and reality was beginning to settle in on Mike too. He was not sure what to do. What do you do when someone has been to Hell? He wanted to go get some intercessors, but as he tried to leave a renewed panic entered me. I didn't want him to leave until I could be free from the unforgiveness inside of me, and then what about the unforgiveness toward others? The amount of panic and stress was escalating and spilling onto Mike.

Mike tried to tell me going to Hell was just God's gift to help others. This caused a reaction that he was not ready for. I assured him that he would go to Hell with me because of the unforgiveness inside of him. To say I turned into a hysterical mess is an understatement. Mike has never had to deal with such a desperate, emotional, panicked person. Nor does he ever desire to do it again! He was trapped with me and he had absolutely no idea what was going on or how to help. He was now a victim too.

At some point I looked into Mike's eyes. There it was—compassion. I saw that Mike would help me and protect me. That is when the explanation of it all started coming out in an unintelligent way. The more I spoke, the more agitated and panicked I became. Mike laid me down in our bed. I didn't want to lie down. What if I went to sleep and woke up in Hell? What if I didn't forgive all the people I needed to? I had no idea how much time I had. Mike needed to understand that it would happen to him, to our children, to our family, and to our friends. To everyone who was harboring unforgiveness.

He insisted that I lie down. I insisted that he lie down on top of me. He had the presence of God in him, and I did not have His presence. I knew that I would die without it. I wanted Mike to cover my whole body to stop it from falling apart and dying like it did in Hell. I was sure that my body was going to begin transforming back into the grotesque one I had in Hell.

Mike tried to assure me that I was fine. I told him then that I would never be fine again, and really that statement was true. I have never returned to the woman I was before I went to Hell.

I kept repeating how I was going to go back to Hell and every time Mike assured me otherwise. I was yelling and angry at him, which scared me more. This was not righteous anger and I knew it would invite the presence of Hell on the earth in the same way that worship invites the presence of God. He tried to assure me, but as I yelled the Scriptures at him I could feel that he had no clue of the assurance. He was faking.

I called him a liar. I told him that he was one of the many people who had hurt me and that because of my unforgiveness toward him and others I would have to return to Hell. My brain was stuck on a wheel and wouldn't stop.

My mind was not on my side. I kept replaying. God had sent me to Hell? *Why* was I more dangerous than the next gal? And what if He realized I was back from Hell? What did I have that I could beg and bargain with Him to let me stay? Added to that was the huge battle looming up ahead—who would believe me?

But my most immediate fear was that I was going to go back to Hell. I feared that at any moment, gates would appear and I would be sucked out of this reality into that one, never to return.

I tried desperately to figure out how to forgive. I had no clue. I had done the thing I thought was forgiveness—pretending like it hadn't happened and never bringing it up. But I knew this wasn't enough. I began to cry but the tears wouldn't come out. Just a raw crying with a voice that was almost gone.

PAIN

Within 24 hours of coming back from Hell, sores filled the inside of my nose. My eyes were burned like when I had flashed them while welding years before. I had sties all over my inner eyelids and I was losing my eyelashes.

Oh, my body hurt! I had all the symptoms of being dehydrated—extreme muscle aches, chronic fatigue, severe headache and brain fog, irritability and irrational fear, insomnia, cracked skin and lips, and the list went on. I couldn't move easily. My bones seemed like they were still grinding against each other as if there were no water inside of me. That was only the beginning of many personal health issues that are too private to share.

My mind would not stop whirling about the unforgiveness in me or how it was going to take me back to Hell. I was terrified of God and unable to pray. By far the worst thing I felt was no God inside me. Today I believe that the amount of panic in me made me unable to feel His presence.

To compensate, the thing I wanted most was to be close to other people. I wanted them to hold me so that I could feel the God inside of them. God made us to fit together. We don't have to trust everyone but we do need to trust someone. It is people who hurt us and it is people who help fix us.

For the next six days I was insane. I did not sleep, which made my mind weaker. I would tell Mike, my children, and my friends, "Oh my God, I'm going to go back to Hell!" I knew all the sins that I had done. How could I be re-forgiven? I knew all the unforgiveness that I had held inside. I knew it had ahold of me and that my desire to let go was not an option.

All of these things tied me to Hell and I had no idea how I was going to cut them off of me. The only idea that came to me was that I needed a sword! I needed a sword of the Spirit to cut this stuff off of me! (See Ephesians 6:17.) I used to have one but I didn't know if I still did.

I asked others to ask God to help me. I was still too afraid to ask for myself. A dear friend sat with me for hours over those six days holding my hands and letting me tell her again and again about all the pain. I really didn't have words. Just mostly tears and fear. She would pray over me and assure me that God was *my* good Father. I didn't believe her, but I wanted her to keep telling me until I could. She was so patient and kind, telling me again and again *you're not going to go back there.*

The question in me: Why did God send me there? The only answer I had was because it is where we all belong when we openly choose to disobey Jesus and disrespect His blood.

Years ago I woke up during a surgery. I was in so much pain! The nurse who was standing up by my head began stroking my face, stared into my eyes, and said "Laurie, honey, it is going to stop hurting in just a minute. Listen to me, look at me, you are going to be okay."

That pain was nothing compared to the pain my body felt in Hell. My mind was so sure that I was going back. I would think on a pain from there and it would manifest itself in my physical body. I wasn't still burning, but

I would still feel it. I hurt everywhere remembering how my body didn't have any water in it. Having no God inside is extremely excruciatingly painful! Thinking on it was a torture but I couldn't stop thinking and I couldn't go to sleep. The longer I was away from Hell, the more I was sure that God was going to find me and send me back.

REPRIEVE

On the sixth night I finally slept. On day seven I woke up and something amazing shifted. All the pain that was in my mind and body was gone. All was calm. My mind was not tormented that I was returning to Hell. It was, for lack of a better understanding, empty. I really liked this!

My body no longer hurt every time I moved. The sties in my eyes were gone, my voice was normal, breathing didn't hurt, and my heart seemed to beat normally again. The other issues seemed to have stopped as well, and I was hungry.

I wanted to see my grandbabies, lie down and take a nap in the sun, and listen to worship music. I wanted to just "be."

I had entered a reprieve. I didn't know what it was, but I was thankful and so I slept a lot. I did not go to church, read my Bible, or pray. I only listened to worship music. I fell in love with Christian instrumental music. Still, when life is too complicated, I love to listen to this music. It seems to remove all the need for words and let my heart just rest.

I wasn't sure if I was still hiding from God, but I felt that He had lifted a burden that was too great for me and I needed to be still and know that He is God (see Ps. 46:10). I knew that soon I would enter into something new. I didn't know what the new thing would be, but it didn't send me into panic. It was like I was in a boxing ring with an opponent. I wasn't sure if it was God or the Devil, but the bell had rung and I was allowed to rest. So I did.

CHAPTER 9

HEALING FROM HELL

WHERE TO BEGIN?

What do you do after you have seen and felt *God* rend His garments against you? What do you do after seeing the price for dishonoring the blood of Jesus in order to live life your own way? What do you do after the agonizing, never-ending burning?

The first six days after going to Hell was all panic! My new normal wasn't much better.

I struggled to sleep. What if I didn't wake up? Instead I paced and I left every light in our house on because I was now afraid of the dark.

I couldn't eat. Worry and fearful thoughts tied my stomach in knots and kept me in a constant state of nausea.

I couldn't watch TV, listen to the radio, or listen to people.

I couldn't think. There was only one thought: *When am I going back to Hell?* I tried to think of anything else. But that one belief dominated my thinking.

Every day, the clock would either never seem to move as I stared at it, waiting for the time to pass, or I would zone out, consumed with who I needed to forgive and an hour would pass in the blink of an eye.

PTSD

A few months after my experience, Mike took me to the hospital because I was experiencing an array of increasingly serious health issues. While there, they diagnosed me with Post Traumatic Stress Disorder (PTSD). It was so upsetting.

The doctors asked if something terrible had happened to me recently to cause the panic. They offered some choices—being held at gunpoint, being raped, a divorce, or the death of a child. All of these are terrible life circumstances and I have deep sympathy for friends and family who have suffered these things.

I answered the doctor, "Yes, I went to Hell!"

They sent in a new doctor to do a psychiatric exam. I passed. Over the next months I had a total of three of those exams. I passed all of them. I have been told time and again by people who hear my story that I am crazy. The trauma I experienced in Hell rarely receives the same compassion that I would receive had I been held at gunpoint or raped or lost a child. When I came back from Hell, there was a room full of people who knew and saw my distress. They told others who were not there, and as the story spread most people had no idea of the trauma associated with the experience. Instantly, I was labeled a weirdo.

OPINIONS

Everyone who heard my experience had an opinion. Some people were very excited for me. They felt as if God had given me a costly gift.

Some asked for the "scoop" like they were going to get a juicy story. I remember a friend asked me to give her the "quick" version of everything that happened. Unfortunately for both of us, I lost it with her. I lectured and yelled at her.

"Hell is not a good teaching! Like you could buy the 'been there done that' T-shirt or something. Are you crazy? People are tormented night and day with no way out and *many, many* people will go there."

I couldn't stop myself. I warned her that everyone had better be very sure that they were right with God because He is more serious about sin than you can imagine.

Whoever unknowingly asked me about it always ended up a part of my breakdown. Awkward!

Also, there were people who wanted to tell me that they didn't believe one word of it. In my confusion and panic, I felt as if I needed to convince them. I was terrified because I thought that if I wasn't believable, then who would help me?

Some who heard my story declared that I must be a Jezebel. She is the only one who was/is unsaveable. Of course, that heaped despair on top of my confusion, panic, and fear.

Lastly, there was my support system who prayed and fasted for me. They found instrumental music and brought light homemade soups hoping they would soothe my stomach. They desired to love me but I was in lockdown. However, they pressed on and took me for walks in the sunlight, showed me pictures of baby animals and children, and shared so many children's jokes (my favorites).

LONGING FOR GOD

My life and thoughts were scattered and scrambled, fragmented and fearful, desperate and exasperating as depression waited to overtake me. When I tried to rest, I was overcome by thoughts of shame, worry, and doubt. I desperately desired to be good enough for God but I *knew* I wasn't good enough for Him. I found no rest. There is no rest outside of *God!* I knew this better now than ever before. There is no rest unless it comes from the Prince of Peace. Salvation brought rest. I had no idea how glorious it was until I entered into it at my salvation. I appreciated it when it came and noticed the remarkable difference, but I didn't appreciate its life-altering value until it was gone.

All this time, I just knew I was going back to Hell. It was what I deserved. I would plead into the air wondering if anyone could hear me.

"Please," I begged of God, "teach me how to talk to You again. How do I pray? Can You still hear me? Can You ever accept me, Lord? I need to know, like I used to, if I am going to be with You where You are! Oh Jesus, my sweet Jesus, can it ever be the same between us? Can I ever be a friend to my Savior again?"

The pain of longing overwhelmed me because I remembered the times I had run into His presence with such confidence. Now those memories were just an unending ache in my heart. I couldn't remember how to run or where His presence was. How would I ever make it to Heaven? The pile of sins that surrounded me while I burned was so great a pile. How could my life ever be free from unforgiveness? Can God accept someone back after He rends His garments?

I began searching for others who had been to Hell. There are many. I met with anyone who had gone to Hell and I always asked the same question—what do you do with the torment? But each person reported a different result. I didn't meet anyone who could tell me that they still suffered from torment. Everyone had reconnected to God almost immediately. This brought me both comfort and distress. Comfort because they did reconnect after Hell but distress because my heart was still lost. Maybe I would never be found or perhaps too much time was passing. I tried not to think this way, to pretend that everything was okay. However, inside I knew nothing was okay. Life without God was not worth living. But dying without God was unthinkable. I was exhausted, sick, stressed, and on a downward spiral.

The list of questions I had no answers for kept growing. Do I talk about having been to Hell to get it out or just live with it all by myself? There was no way to keep it bottled inside! Mike and I thought that if I could tell some people, maybe find some language for it, that this would help me. But when I talked about it I got stuck in the horrific memories. I had flashbacks that caused their own set of complications and health problems.

We were not prepared for the physical, mental, and emotional stress that talking about it placed on me. It was a reset to the reality of Hell and how much unforgiveness was still in me. The one thing I could be thankful about in the retelling was that it always reminded me of the areas that needed work in my heart. As I recalled Hell, I remembered the sins of unforgiveness piled in my chamber. I recalled each one, dealt with the pain, and opened my heart for not only revealing the truth but for cleansing and healing. It was not a quick fix like I wanted. Instead, it took time and energy and it hurt again as if it had just happened.

We learned quickly that we needed intercessors covering me in prayer each time I shared about my time in Hell. As I spoke, God gave me language to explain something I had experienced, usually as a comparison.

Finally, we figured if we could record me talking about it, then other people could be warned and I wouldn't have to tell the story over and over, causing trauma each time. The first several sound recordings were all blank—there was no sound on playback. We tried video recordings but neither the sound nor the picture worked.

We gathered the intercessors again and prayed to find a way to get the thing recorded. We wanted to help people if that were possible. Everyone needed the truth of what the Bible says about Hell. A team of people came around us including videographers with backup cameras, intercessors, ministers and people who came to listen. I had a good friend give a biblical teaching on Hell before I spoke. It was perfect because my experience lined up with what is in the Bible about Hell and it helped all of us understand.

Afterward, I was exhausted. The ministry team was overwhelmed. There were many people who needed help to be free of sin.

RESPONSES TO HELL

Those who heard my story processed it in one of several ways:

The first response was, *"You are a liar! Christians don't go to Hell. It's not real. You are a fake. You had a bad dream and now you are pushing this off onto God. You need to repent for lying. You will go to Hell for sharing this."*

This is the response from people who are trapped in fear and unbelief. The idea of a good God having a place like Hell for "bad" people is outside their understanding of God. Therefore, it must not be true and that makes me a liar. They believe that Heaven is based on doing good things and everyone has done something good, right?

They like to add statements like: *"Talking about Hell does not glorify Jesus, and only glorifies you!"* As if I created Hell in a bad dream, a hallucination, or that I invented a story of going to Hell for attention.

When I point them to scriptures that verify the truth of Hell as a real place that I experienced, they begin to walk in manipulation of the scriptures. Taking the blessings of the scriptures and ignoring the warnings and curses. They say ridiculous things like, *"If your God sends people to Hell, then I want nothing to do with a God like Him!"*

If they are willing, I meet with them and listen to their arguments, which always include their individual ideas of what God should do. They desire to ban the reality of Hell and create a false grace message where everyone goes to Heaven, if not immediately, with time or with prayers for them. They create many ways for God to change so that their plans will work. They create a new God as if they are more compassionate and righteous than He is. I tell them, *"You don't have to believe me. However, we all have to believe Jesus. And Jesus has spoken loud and clear about Hell in His Scriptures."*

The second response is, *"Oh my God, my family is going to go to Hell! It's real? What can I do?"*

This group of people has been asleep regarding the reality of where their family and friends are at spiritually. They are the group that allows compromise, snubs holiness as if it is old-fashioned, and lowers the bar that Jesus set so that their loved ones are qualified. They look the other way, make excuses, and even defend sin. They know who God is but have allowed the sinful times to cloud their judgment and opened their hearts to human concessions. They believe that everyone is in sin; therefore, who are we to call anyone to holiness?

I realized that all of us allow compromise for others. We move the standard of holiness so we or someone we love can still be okay. I have done this before as if I am more generous than Jesus. But it gets us so far from what God originally set forth.

I've been accused of trying to manipulate the testimony of Hell to hurt, trouble, scare, and panic people's feelings so that they would not live separated from God. The Bible is clear and there is enough information about sin and how it separates us from a loving God. In fact the Bible teaches we should "fear" God (see Deut. 6:24; Ps. 112:1; 115:13; 128:1-4; Prov. 19:23; 22:4; Rev. 11:18). That should make us all serious about what the Bible really says regarding sin and Hell.

Again, I tell this group, *"You don't have to believe me, but you do have to believe Jesus."* If we don't have His saving blood for our sins, we cannot enter His Kingdom. The truth is that everyone has sinned and everyone is headed for Hell except for the ones who follow, trust, love, and obey Jesus.

Another response was, *"Pray for me that God would take me to Hell."*

Honestly, I have no patience for this group. I can understand the others. Hell and its realities are too ghastly to believe. Also, I understood that when we realize there is unforgiveness in our hearts, it is scary to face. If someone believed once saved, always saved, of course they would argue. But asking for God to take you to Hell? It is a ridiculous and dangerous request! I prayed that they would stop admiring the darkness, love Jesus more, and bask in the glory of our Lord to be safe and content in Him.

It is important to pause here and share that I no longer believe "once saved, always saved." Maybe I did at one time, but the reality of Hell changed that. Seeing Christian people in Hell has caused me to search the Bible for the truth that I now see clearly. Actually, the number-one question I get about Hell is why I went there. But the number-two question is why I don't believe in "once saved, always saved."

You see, I was purchased by Jesus with the only acceptable price—innocent shed blood. I am a slave of the cross. Or as I tell people, Jesus is the boss. I no longer get to do what I want. I do what He wants. And after walking as a slave to Jesus for some time, I discovered that He saved me so that I can be His family, His sister, His daughter. Amazing! But it gets better—Jesus desires me to rule and reign with Him as the Bride of Christ. *Unbelievable!*

Therefore, *never* should Jesus ever have to remind me that I am His slave and that I should obey Him.

The "once saved, always saved" concept is only a half truth, making it a lie. It is absolutely true with regard to Jesus' work. What He purchased is finished and can never be redone, reopened, or disputed. In that aspect, "once saved, always saved" is absolutely true. Jesus died for mankind to be saved and it will always be the perfect sacrifice. Jesus completed His side of the equation, and it was and is perfect (see John 19:30).

"Once saved, always saved," however, does not stand up biblically when it implies that as a saved person I can sin willfully, keep sinning willfully, and believe that the agreement entered into with Jesus toward obedience covers all the disobedience/sin without continued repentance.

On the first day that Jesus saved me, He saved me from all the sin of my past right up to that very moment. I was not guilty of any sin. He set a precedent that I can rely on. Now the next time I sinned, I had an understanding of how to go to Jesus and be forgiven and walk out sanctification. But until I ask for forgiveness of this sin, I am still guilty of it. It is not automatically covered because of the first time Jesus forgave me when He saved me.

Let me give you an example. I have a friend who was struggling in his marriage with his wife. He cheated on her and demanded a divorce. She did not want a divorce. She wanted to fight for her marriage and was willing to go to marriage counseling. Her husband refused to end the relationship with the other woman, to agree to counseling, or to work it out.

I met with him and went over what the Bible says,

> *Now the works of the flesh are evident, which are: adultery, fornication, uncleanness, lewdness, idolatry, sorcery, hatred, contentions, jealousies, outbursts of wrath, selfish ambitions, dissensions, heresies, envy, murders, drunkenness, revelries, and the like; of which I tell you beforehand, just as I also told you in time past, that those who practice such things will not inherit the kingdom of God* (Galatians 5:19-21).

I pointed out that he was in an adulterous relationship. I showed him scriptures that say that it is sinful to cheat on your wife or divorce her. He didn't care. He believed that on the day (back in the 1980s) when he received Jesus as his Savior, Jesus forgave him from every sin whether he wanted to make this one right or not. My friend is walking in deception.

Sin still separates us from God. And the best thing we can do is run to the cross of Jesus and let Him have His way. So, first you are saved, then you are sanctified through obedience to the Scriptures. According to John MacArthur, the sanctification process includes three steps: cognition, conviction and affection. Jesus said in John 14:15, *"If you love me, obey me"* (TLB)

The last response I received after telling my testimony was, *"Oh my God, I'm filled with unforgiveness and I'm going to Hell."*

For this group of people there is immediate hope. Jesus forgave us of everything. He forgives. We receive it with a repentant heart. Repentance means four things.

1. Understanding sin according to God. We agree with what He says is sin.

2. Godly sorrow for sin we have committed. More than just feeling sorry but feeling deep remorse.

3. Willingness to make restitution. How sorrowful are we? Willing to do whatever it takes to make it right?

4. Putting something in place to not sin again. And if you do the same sin again, then the thing you put in place the last time didn't work, so put something new and more reliable in place to stop sinning.

Jesus teaches, *"And do not fear those who kill the body but cannot kill the soul. But rather fear Him who is able to destroy both soul and body in hell"* (Matt. 10:28). He's telling us don't fear man, but fear God.

Nothing Like Hell

As time went on, I looked ahead on the calendar and I was overtaken by a new fear. The first anniversary was fast approaching. What if all I had was a year to clean up my life? My panic came back full force. A dear friend knew how deeply I struggled. She told me to look at August 28th as a celebration day. I was sure she was not my friend to say that. Who could ask me to celebrate the day God took me to Hell? I was sure she didn't have a clue what she was saying!

However, she bought Mike and me tickets for a train ride which is something I had always wanted to do. She paid for us to stay overnight in another town so I could be ready to receive, as she called it, a unique quiet experience from the Lord on the day I dreaded to face. I was numb as I went through the day. But for Mike, so many things went wrong. We were cold, wet, hungry, and worn out from all the walking we did. On the outside, it looked like a really terrible day. And in the middle of the mess, I understood. It wasn't Hell. It didn't matter how bad anything was, it was not Hell.

People say, "I've had a hellish day." No, they didn't. The principles of Hell are *not* on the earth because God has never completely left us. He is still working on the earth. But He isn't in Hell. It took me 365 days to realize this earth is not Hell because God *is* here. On that day, I let go of depending on the love of God in others to be the only God that I felt around me. Instead, I grabbed on to the reality that the love of God is everywhere on the earth.

WHERE WAS GOD?

After the one-year anniversary my emotions became a roller coaster. The enemy was always whispering—how could a loving God allow anyone to go to Hell? Those and many other demonic thoughts tried to get me to question everything. Grace, trust, mercy, eternity—these are Heaven words. They can only be defined by God. But the doubts made me question every good thing of God and His Kingdom, including those Heaven words. I also questioned if I had ever really been to Heaven or Hell and if it really mattered.

One day I discussed with Mike the fact that I knew God had not been with me in Hell. This idea troubled me greatly. Mike reminded me of when our girls were one and three. We lived in an apartment where the community laundry room was just below our place. I put the girls down for a nap and hurried down to get a load going. No sooner had I started loading the wash than I heard our three-year-old's feet patter across her bedroom and into the kitchen. I hurriedly shoved the laundry and soap in and started the machine and then rushed back upstairs in time to hear my daughter talking on the phone. I assumed she was pretending to talk to her grandma, which she loved to do. I put the phone up to my ear and discovered she was actually talking to the emergency responder who said the authorities were on their way to my house. Then the police, fire department, and social services showed up at my door. In the few minutes I was downstairs, she had dialed 0 and told the operator she was alone taking care of her baby sister. In that moment, she had believed she was completely alone because she couldn't see me. Once I explained the situation to the authorities and they investigated my home, all was fine.

Mike told me that only God could have opened the door of Hell to let me out. He gently reminded me that even though I didn't see God in Hell, He had never left me. This was my second unique quiet experience with God. I had a knowing that what God said was true: *"He will never leave you nor forsake you"* (Deut. 31:6 NIV).

During this time, I tried to connect to the Bible. It had always been a source of encouragement, direction, and strength, but now the Bible was filled *everywhere* with truths about Hell. Book after book reminded me of my experience. The Gospels had once been my favorites. Now, I could only hear all the warnings. I stopped reading it. Why had I never seen all of those verses before? I think it was because I didn't want to. I wanted Hell to be a place for Satan and his demons. Hell is that, but it is also the place where *everyone* is going because of sin. Everyone except for those who choose to *obey* Jesus.

I knew there was safety in the Word of God, so I would just repeat to myself the verse that talked about Jesus being good to sinners.

> *The Son of Man came eating and drinking, and they say,*
> *"Look, a glutton and a winebibber, a friend of tax collectors*
> *and sinners!"* (Matthew 11:19)

I also held on dearly to:

Little children, you are from God and have overcome them, for he who is in you is greater than he who is in the world (1 John 4:4 ESV).

Be strong and courageous. Do not be afraid or terrified because of them, for the Lord your God goes with you; he will never leave you nor forsake you (Deuteronomy 31:6 NIV).

If God had ever come to live inside me, and I knew He had, then He would not leave me because God cannot lie. If God ever didn't do what He said, then everything would stop existing. I understood, not perfectly, but I understood that God is so bound by His own words that even He is accountable to them.

In my crisis, I clung to a few people. In the beginning, they checked up on me often. With time, they started to grow weary of my same questions. I would ask them countless times if they thought that I would make it to Heaven when I die. I would ask them why God had sent me to Hell. Always their answers were certain that God, our Father, loved me and still wanted me in Heaven with Him and that Jesus loved me and sent me to Hell so that I would warn others. Even though I had asked and their answers were exactly what I wanted to hear, there was still no peace. I could not put my hope in their assurances. I needed the assurance that I once had—the assurance of salvation, acceptance, love, and eternity straight from my Father. Assurance was hopelessly missing, seemingly forever. But what could I do, where could I go? Who else had the words of life or was willing to save me? I felt like Peter when Jesus asked him if he was going to leave. He answered, "Where else would I go?" (see John 6:68).

BECAUSE I LOVE YOU

I struggled with worship. Was my worship real? I heard once that the majority of the worship is all about the worshiper wanting to be seen by men and that this kind of worship disgusts God. I have given that type of worship before, maybe too much. But how is it that we get to abandonment? Should I sit quietly, stand out of respect, yell, go to the altar, or just drop to my knees? How was my worship before I went to Hell? Today, was my worship really for Him, or was it now a performance in hopes that I could get something from Him? *Yes*, I wanted something from Him. I wanted Him! Why did I have to always think so much? I hurt somewhere deep at the memory that worship used to allow me to enter into abandonment and intimacy with Jesus. I felt that the open door to Hell had closed my door to worship.

Before I went to Hell, church was one of my favorite places. To me, it was a wonderful place where belonging to a global "family" gathering was all to bless the Lord. Upon being saved, church was a gathering that I fit into instantly and perfectly. Once, when I was first saved, I was at church on a terribly snowy day. One of the oldest members of our church arrived with his walker and made it gingerly across the wet, slippery concrete floors to the front row where he always sat. I suggested to him that days like that were good ones for him to stay toasty warm and safe inside his home. He gently and firmly corrected me. He explained how he would always come to church on the Lord's Day to see his great God and Father and to be seen by Him. He taught me that we belong in the presence of God, and that being at church would sustain us in ways that we couldn't get anywhere else. He said that God needed me and that I needed Him. Being at church was the time we both got our needs met. I believed that faithful man and lived it out each week.

However, now I struggled with Sundays and going to church. God was at church. And when I went, I knew He would see me. I knew I would come under the scornful eye of Heaven, so church became a painful mind game. I watched the clock, feeling guilty the whole time and wishing that the worship would end so that the message, which always pertained to my guilt, could also end. Then I could leave the house of the Lord and His disappointment in me. I was so guilty. I felt just like when I went to church as a lost person. I remembered feeling like an outsider in church and around Christians. I knew that feeling came from believing I didn't belong—that I was without salvation. I was sure that I was not desired by my Father God in His Kingdom any longer.

But one Sunday, something was different. The longing in me to get away from the pain was deeper than the guilt and shame. My desperation so filled me and I was overcome by the feeling that someone was reaching out with a light of hope. During worship they asked for anyone who wanted prayer to come to the altar. I went. Guilty people find rest at the altar. I knew this as a fisher of men and have used that truth before to help people answer an altar call. While I was there, I received prayer from a woman I highly respect and then I returned to my seat.

I didn't try to sing or engage. I just sat down. To my relief, I started weeping. I had long since stopped sweetly weeping and only found desperate crying as a companion. But that day, as the weeping began, I can only explain that a heavy thing was set upon me. It wasn't a painful heavy but a weight of security. Then, as the pastor began his message, I heard the voice of God, my Good Father, speaking through the heaviness into each cell of my being, "I sent you to Hell because I love you!"

It was the first time my spirit had felt safe since Hell. The heavy feeling was God and it was different than any presence I had ever felt before. It safely immobilized me. It touched everything. I felt as if my blood had stopped moving and it was exactly right. The only part of me that was working were the tears streaming out of my eyes.

I am a warrior! I know that when I am under attack I must quickly snap into action. I know that while I am in a fight, I cannot let my guard down. Instead, I quickly pull out my sword and shield in the spirit and wait or fight. I make no fast decisions until I feel the Holy Spirit tell me what to do, see the help He has sent, or hear Him give the all clear. I know that I must wait long enough and do what He tells me to do so together we will win!

Once years ago, before the new types of ceiling-fan mounts, I was standing on a ladder with my arms above my head holding on to a ceiling fan while Mike was on another ladder installing the wires up into the ceiling. Holding was easier for me than connecting. I was holding with all I had, but soon my muscles began to shake and then burn. When Mike finally got the wires attached and took the heavy thing from me there was such a relief that rushed over my whole body, a relief that I hadn't fallen off the ladder or dropped the fan, that I could put my burning arms down and that the task was accomplished.

This heavy security of the Lord was the all clear. I could let my guard down. Oh the relief! The relief of the Holy Spirit heaviness wrapping around my whole body, mind, will, emotions, and spirit was a suddenly, a healing time, and a connection. God was connecting many ties from me to Himself that had been broken while I burned. My sword and shield no longer needed to be up for battle. I had no idea that I had been holding them since my experience or that I was still fighting. I had been holding on for exactly 30 months—waiting, fighting, crying, guilty, doubting, exposed, fearful, and isolated but still His.

During all that time, I never wanted to let go of who Jesus is and all He represents. I had almost given in, but the reality was that I never left Him even in the face of great confusion, great offense, and very small spiritual understanding. My warrior spirit was still waiting on my Savior when He came to relieve me. There was not a loud celebration. Only my deeply raw and infected wounds exposed, cleansed, bound up, and heavily smothered. For the first time in 30 months, I felt welcomed and reconnected.

Still, the only thing that moved was my tears. I just sat in the heaviness willing my body to never move, to never leave this place, to stay in His presence. As I sat in love, understanding came. It was nice of Him to give understanding, but it didn't matter. The only thing that mattered was that I was His.

I want to always be fine with the truth that I don't understand everything. On this side of Heaven I can only understand in part. Like through a glass dimly. It is enough that my Father wanted me to know that it was He who sent me to Hell. I knew that He would explain in the right time, but for then it was enough to know that He was in control. There was a reason and it was because He loved *me!* He still loves me, never stopped loving me, and never will. Like a child having a broken bone reset, I can trust that my Father is only doing me good no matter how much it hurts me. In the words of Job, *"Even though He slay me, yet will I trust Him"* (Job 13:15).

Today, as I recall this moment my heart explodes again! My Father speaks to the desperate. He will never let me endure more than I can handle because He will never leave me or forsake me (see Deut. 31:8). He will always rescue His warriors, children, and friends. He knows my breaking point.

It took a very long time to overcome the panic of Hell—30 months exactly. I have studied the number 30, but I realize that I will probably not fully comprehend that length of time until I stand before Him. On this side of healing after Hell and knowing my Father and His care for me, I realize that it doesn't matter that it took that long. On this side of having a heart that is fully liberated from unforgiveness, there is freedom from any of the worry. *"This is how my heavenly Father will treat each of you unless you forgive your brother or sister from your heart"* (Matt. 18:35 NIV).

On this side of healing from Hell are security and assurance of eternity. There is a passion inside of me to help people inside the Church and the lost meet Jesus on His terms. My eternal perspective is to obey Jesus and set an example that my children, grandchildren, friends, neighbors, co-workers, and the people I evangelize can follow.

Now to answer the questions that I began this chapter with.

What do you do after you have seen and felt God rend His garments against you?

If I had died in that vision, I believe I would be eternally in Hell. Jesus let me see and experience the reality of Hell first, for my own freedom, and second, so that I could tell you. Hell is a real place and there are really people there in torment beyond my earthly words. There is nothing any of those people in Hell can do now that God has torn His garments. They are now separated from His heart forever. The biblical meaning of rending your garments is a sign of grief, mourning, and extreme loss.

The Bible says, *"Then Jacob tore his clothes, put sackcloth on his waist, and mourned for his son many days"* (Gen. 37:34). This is when he thought that Joseph had been killed. Tearing the clothes over the heart was an act done when something was dead. When there was no hope. There is no hope for the people in Hell. And the pain this causes God is something we can never understand.

The Lord hurts over the agony of His creation being separated from Him. However, His hurt is magnified many, many times more than this weak comparison.

> *"Even now,"* declares the Lord, *"return to me with all your heart, and with fasting, weeping and mourning; and **rend your heart and not your garments."** Return to the Lord your God, for he is gracious and compassionate, slow to anger, abounding in love, and he relents from sending calamity* (Joel 2:12-13 NIV).

All of us need to rend our hearts for the times we have chosen disobedience, disrespect, and hatred against the only person who does everything thinkable to bring us to Himself. Without God we are on a path to eternal separation. It makes sense that He would rend His garments at the great loss of His beautiful creation.

For me, I will rend my heart. I will get away from sin and warn others of its horrible outcome!

What do you do after seeing the price for dishonoring the blood of Jesus in order to live life your own way?

The price for not accepting Jesus on His terms is eternal separation. The place for separation is Hell. It was created as the place away from God, the place without the presence of God. It was created for Satan and the demons. Satan is the master of sin and sin separates us from God. *Everyone* is guilty of sin! We are all in need of the only acceptable sacrifice for sin—innocent shed blood. The way of the Lord is holiness and holiness is being with God. None of us can achieve holiness on our own. Therefore, we need a Savior who can rescue us from the penalty of sin. There is only one name under Heaven by which men must be saved and His name is *Jesus* (see Acts 4:12). Only He has the holy price to pay for sin. His holy blood is the price needed to purchase us out of sin.

On this side of eternity, we must realize, accept, and *respect* the Savior and His blood. We must obey Jesus! We dishonor God when we dishonor the blood of Jesus or water down His ways, requests, and requirements as if by doing this He will modify His plans. Our God *never* changes! He is the same yesterday, today, and forever (see Heb. 13:8). Forever, Jesus' bloodshed for our sin is the only way to eternal *life*.

Have you ever been so grateful that you didn't get what you deserved? That a different outcome was given to you instead of the doom that was imminent?

Many years ago when our oldest daughter was a baby, there was an accident. I was heating up a bottle on the stove. Back then we used glass bottles and placed them in a pan of water until the formula inside heated up. I held her in my arms as she was very fussy and I hoped that the bottle would calm her. Unfortunately, I left the bottle on too long and the water was boiling. At the same time that I grabbed the scalding hot bottle from the water with one hand, she pushed with her legs against my side. In my attempt to keep the boiling water and bottle away from her, she flipped out of my arms and onto the floor. She began screaming immediately. I was distraught!

We rushed her to the hospital because I just knew something was not right. It is a long story so I will skip to the point. She had a brain injury that I knew I had caused. The medical staff were discussing her prognosis and it was dim. After hearing it all, I went to the chapel where I am sure there was an angel sent to help me.

The man, or angel, helped me pray to God for His favor and outcome. I felt a peace sweep over me that removed all the remorse and guilt and instilled a certainty that everything was going to be okay. I went up to her room to share with Mike about the experience. When the doctors came in later, they were amazed at the transformation. She was going to be just fine.

I was and am so grateful to God for fixing the wrong things. He altered a terrible circumstance and allowed our daughter to grow up safe and whole. We are so grateful, even today, that we can never forget the great thing He did for us and for her.

How is it then, that after my experience in Hell, I could ever take for granted the holy blood that saved my daughter and has done so much more for me? After seeing the fires of Hell, I have a renewed awe to live my life holy and for Jesus! My gratitude is great but I desire that it would increase every day. I ask the Lord to show me the wonderful things He is doing in my life so I can walk in thankfulness and deep indebtedness. I believe that this heart posture is the answer for thinking that we can live our lives without His direction and guidance.

Jesus doesn't have to do one more thing for me to love Him. He has done the greatest thing with the power of His holy blood. I will live in thankful obedience and I will warn as many people about sin as will listen before it is too late!

What do you do after the agonizing, never-ending burning?

I feel as if I was given a second chance. Maybe everyone in Hell was given a second chance, a visitation, or a time to repent. I am positive that it hurts God above everything to be separated from us.

> *The Lord is not slow to fulfill his promise as some count slowness, but is patient toward you, not wishing that any should perish, but that all should reach repentance* (2 Peter 3:9 ESV).

God doesn't want *anyone* to perish in Hell. The problem isn't that there is a Hell or that God made it for Satan and the demons. The problem is that we don't believe that God should let people choose if they want to live with Him or not. We act as if God is mean or bad because people are in Hell. As if He should do something more. When in reality God has done *everything* for our good.

I live my life very differently since I experienced the burning in Hell. I take all sin very seriously. We all should. I do not sin like I used to. I do not sin as often as I used to, and I do not make excuses for it in my life or in the lives of others.

Since burning, I pray for revival and put my energy into being used by God to snatch as many as possible from Hell. I don't think I will ever forget what I felt, saw, smelled, heard, and tasted. I still panic when I talk about Hell. I think this is a good and normal response. However, the topic is taboo in most circles.

One time I went to a new salon to get my nails done. The owner, a nice lady, was helping me and asked if it was for a special occasion. I said it was. She wanted to know what type of event I was going to. I explained that I was going to be sharing about a life-changing event and how I wanted to stack the deck in my favor for confidence. Nice outfit, new shoes, updated hairstyle, and, of course, pretty nails.

She wanted to know if it was a wedding. I shared that it was maybe more important than a wedding. I told her that I have had many spiritual experiences and one of the most important ones was my experience in Hell. She was shocked.

When I asked her if she has what she needs to go to Heaven, she told me that she never allows talk of religion or politics in her salon. I smiled and asked her, "You know who made that rule don't you?" She didn't. I told her that Satan made that rule because he doesn't want people to find God or implement His ways. So I asked again if she had what she needed to go to Heaven. She did not. By the time my nails were ready she was prepared to look seriously at the sins that she had committed and the reality that a payment was necessary.

Since Hell, I have a consuming need to get in front of people and point everyone to our great and loving Father who has made a way for us to be with Him where He is. Burning was not created for you or me. We need to tell everyone about Jesus!

PART 3

LESSONS I LEARNED IN HELL

CHAPTER 10

———◆———

HELL HAS NO HUMILITY

SIN AND HUMILITY DO NOT MIX

I had many sleepless nights pondering my experience in Hell. Each one became a gift in searching out truth. My mind raced with all the questions of who, what, when, where, why, and how because of the eternal importance of understanding the principles of Heaven and Hell.

Questions such as: How did sin separate us in the first place? What was Satan after in the garden with Adam and Eve? I knew that if I could grasp even a partial understanding of those questions, then maybe I could understand how sin operated in me.

Our God is a God of humility! I wondered, who was I to even begin to approach such a topic? The Bible has heroes we can study who walked in humility. Jesus is the most perfect example of that virtue. I knew that the opposite of humility is pride, which is simply "doing it my way." The Lord is void of pride! Satan wanted Adam and Eve to abandon humility and embrace pride. And they did. It is something Satan desired from me. The question I faced—was I like Adam and Eve?

It is prideful to think that my ways are more righteous than God's ways or that my words are better than God's (see Isa. 55:9). Therefore, it is extremely prideful to think that my earthly understandings are better than God's decisions. And yet, I did just that time and again. Until I experienced Hell. Pride is everywhere in Hell while humility is nowhere to be found. Because of this reality, it was essential that I understood the importance of humility and the devastation of pride. When I returned from Hell, I set my heart to understand the power of sin.

The Bible teaches that God desires obedience more than sacrifice (see 1 Sam. 15:22). Humility includes obedience. It is a humble thing to walk with God in the way He says we should walk with Him. The truth is that disobedience—or call it what it is, sin—caused such turmoil for all mankind. The solution—humble obedience.

Humility is not something that we can just "know" and we've got it covered. Before Hell, I believed I knew what was right and good for me. This type of knowing was a cover-up for pride. To be humble, we have to practice and practice and then practice some more. It is a choice. Of course, there is a place where God gifts someone in humility, but if God has not gifted us in that way, then we have to *choose* humility, just like we have to choose obedience.

I think about a child growing up. A good parent teaches them to obey. This is such an important pillar for their future. When they are grown they must obey all sorts of things such as speed limits, legal documents, and bosses. As children, we learn a lifestyle of submitting from parents, grandparents, and teachers, which prepares us to trust and obey God.

My visit to Hell could have all been avoided had I obeyed the teaching of Jesus and lived a life of forgiveness.

But!

There is a three letter word that is a powerful enemy of humility: "But!" This seemingly benign word allows us to interpret our situation outside of God's view and change His rules to benefit our situation. I often talk with people who want to share their personal "but" with me.

"But you don't know what they did to me."

What they really are saying is that they shouldn't have to forgive because of the way they were treated. I understand because I, too, have been terribly hurt by others. I understand the pain and suffering at the hands of people who broke earthly and heavenly laws. I understand the breach of trust this causes. If we don't understand the ways of God, it doesn't make sense to do it His way, to forgive. However, often we just want what we want. So we make decisions based on feelings and personal desires and then we attempt to justify it instead of following God's plan.

Years ago when my daughters were in their early teens, we were having a dinner party. Things weren't going right and time was slipping away. I had chosen a very time-consuming recipe that resulted in too many dirty dishes. I had not allowed time to spruce up the house and get myself ready. Then I realized I needed to go to the store to purchase a necessary item. AARRRG. My frustration was high.

I called my daughters in and assigned them tasks. Clean the kitchen, sweep the floors, freshen up the bathroom and then go change your clothes. When I returned our oldest daughter was sweeping out the garage and our youngest was doing poop patrol in the backyard. *What?*

Now you may think what wonderful children I have, but they didn't do what I asked them to do so the good things they did couldn't replace what they should have done. Instead of praising them, I corrected them.

Don't we do this same thing with God? Bringing Him what we *want* to do rather than what He asked for. This is disobedience, which is sin. No good thing is better than obedience to the thing He asked us to do.

Adam and Eve had two famous trees in the garden. There was a Tree of Life that they could eat from. And the other tree that they were never to eat from, the Tree of the Knowledge of Good and Evil. The Tree of Life offered goodness, hope, success, happiness, and so much more. The Tree of the Knowledge of Good and Evil was a mixture that no one would ever be able to handle. The good and evil were intermingled, like an egg with the yolk and the white scrambled together. It makes perfect sense to eat only from the Tree of Life, yet Adam and Eve, being so much like me, chose to try out the other one. Why? What was Satan after?

Humility does not include total understanding or even partial understanding. Humility includes a trust in God that He is good and that He has it figured out. It includes a fierce love that refuses to be disloyal. Humility demands obedience.

Before Adam and Eve ate from the Tree of the Knowledge of Good and Evil, they were righteous. They ate from the Tree of Life and benefited from humility, partnership, love, community, and the list goes on and on. After Adam and Eve ate from the forbidden tree, we all suffer from the knowledge of good and evil. The only way to avoid the ongoing ramifications of sin caused by disobedience is to understand and participate in humility. In other words, trust and obey God.

Sounds much easier than it is. What if God wants something hard?

One time, a pastor asked me to help with the evangelism thrust that they were doing at a local college campus. My job was to help with the altar call. I was waiting just off stage. As the pastor's message wound down, I heard the voice of Jesus speak to me. He said: "Would you like the life of Job?"

What? I recognized His voice and I could tell that He was excited to talk to me about His proposal, but this was *wrong!* All I knew about Job was that God had let Satan do all kinds of terrible things to him and then became angry with Job when he asked God a question. The standard that was set in my heart from sermons I had heard were all about how people better not question God. Frankly, Job and the God he served terrified me. It was a shock to hear Jesus ask me, excitedly nonetheless, if I wanted the life of Job.

I heard it so clearly that I panicked, turned around, and found the closest exit. The back stage door took me outside, but wouldn't let me back in. It was one of those emergency-only exit doors. I was in an emergency.

My husband came out the door yelling for me to stop. He had no idea what was happening. I kept walking away, almost running. When he caught up to me, he was upset. He tried, to no avail, to get me to stop and turn around for the altar call.

I kept yelling at him, "God hates me!" This made no sense to him. We walked all the way back to the house where we were staying. By the time I arrived, I had formulated a plan. Just don't plan on doing altar calls!

If you feel like none of this is making sense, welcome to Mike's confusion. He wanted to know what on the earth had caused me to panic. Didn't I know that that right now the pastor needed me and that God was going to use me?

And Jesus was waiting for an answer. I told Him, "No, I never want the life of Job!"

I was not walking in humility, I was walking in fear.

As the years passed, Jesus' question never left the back of my mind. In my hardest moments over the next two years, I could hear Jesus ask me again, "Would you like the life of Job?"

Job was a humble man and we can learn a lot from him. Mike tried to help me do this. He looked for every teaching he could find about the life of Job. They all freaked me out. I thought what was being asked was just too hard. When I was in Bible college, I joined a group to study it further without anyone knowing that I had been offered the life. I just had no grid for Job, the story, the need for the lessons from the story, or the perfect place of God in it.

My favorite teacher in Bible college taught us that every time we read the Bible and believe that God is the bad guy, the problem is with us, not God. He can never be the bad guy! I took that as the *truth* because Jesus said that if we have seen Him, then we have seen the Father (see John 14:9). Jesus is the exact replication of God the Father.

I knew that I was running out of time to say "yes." Jesus is patient, but He won't wait forever. So I carefully selected the wording of my answer to His question. I said, "Lord, I can't say yes because I am afraid of the Father, but I won't say no. I give You permission to do what is best for me, making sure that I will make it into Heaven."

After Hell, I became intensely ready to look at God the Father through the life of Job. It was the only place I found in Scripture that brought comfort to my stressed-out soul. I answered God the Father, with a new ability to trust, "*Yes*, I want the life of Job!"

Who was Job to our Father God? "*Have you considered My servant Job, that there is none like him on the earth, a blameless and upright man, one who fears God and shuns evil?*" (Job 1:8).

Job is my hero! God was hoping to identify someone for me to pattern my life after. Job was so important to God. He had lived his life in such a way that the Father called him "My servant." The Father declared that Job was His. Wouldn't any of us want that? Jesus is the servant. Job was a forerunner to that title of servant. This is important because there are not many who were like Jesus *before* Jesus.

Satan was walking in some of the heights of his pride. God called on a mere man with a lifestyle of great humility, knowing that Job would not let Him down. God knew the heart of humility that was in Job and that his heart of humility would carry him through the great testing. Job and Satan didn't know the power of the level of humility that Job walked in, but God did. He chose Job, not to beat Satan but to highlight the power of a trusting humility in God. Like I said, Job is my hero!

These are some of the verses that jumped off the page at me after Hell:

> "*Shall we indeed accept good from God, and shall we not accept adversity?*" In all of this Job did not sin with his lips (Job 2:10).

Humility is to speak the things that are true, to keep an eye on my lips and not allow sin. And where does it say that only good things come from the Father? Wasn't the perfect plan for our salvation Jesus Christ dying the most terrible death to purchase men for God?

> *For the thing I greatly feared has come upon me, and what I dreaded has happened to me* (Job 3:25).

What is the worst thing that can happen to you? And what if it does? Is God still God? Jesus asked the Father if there was another way, different from the cross. What Jesus dreaded most happened to Him, and yet the Father used that very dreadful and fearful event to secure our freedom.

> *Therefore do not despise the chastening of the Almighty. For He bruises, but He binds up; He wounds, but His hands make whole* (Job 5:17-18).

I am not immune to being corrected and forcefully stopped by God. What made me think that it wouldn't hurt? Yet, as He was there doing it, why is it that I can't believe that He would help me, heal me, and make me better than new?

> *Then you scare me with dreams and terrify me with visions* (Job 7:14).

Hell is terrifying and yet God has achieved great good from taking me there in a vision. He saved my life and through the telling of it caused many to examine their own hearts and choose forgiveness.

> *Truly I know it is so, but how can a man be righteous before God? If one wished to contend with Him, he could not answer Him one time out of a thousand* (Job 9:2-3).

Who am I to tell God what is good? He can never be the bad guy! At every presentation God would be righteous and me unrighteous.

Though He slay me, yet will I trust Him (Job 13:15).

God is always righteous. Even if God came to kill me, I can trust that His plan is for my good. Like Abraham, who was asked to sacrifice his only son. He obeyed until the Father provided a different sacrifice (see Gen. 22).

Behold, I am vile; what shall I answer You? I lay my hand over my mouth. Once I have spoken, but I will not answer; yes, twice, but I will proceed no further (Job 40:4-5).

There comes a point where we realize that our best answer to God is coming from a broken, sick, and evil frame. Our hearts are wicked. When I stood in His holiness in Heaven, I knew exactly how unholy I was. When I was burning in Hell, I knew how righteous it was for me to be there.

I have heard of You by the hearing of the ear, but now my eye sees You. Therefore I abhor myself, and repent in dust and ashes (Job 42:5-6).

Humility! This statement of Job's to me is proof that his humility was perfected. In fact, after these words the Lord restored Job's losses and the Bible says that God gave to Job twice as much as he had before. And God blessed all the days of Job's life onward.

How does sin separate us? One way is using our way of pride instead of God's way of humility. Anytime Jesus asks us if He can give us something, we need to answer, "*Yes!*" We should answer quickly, assuredly, and confidently! We must not let our finite knowledge turn us away from humility but rather use the practice of this attribute to secure His ways in our lives. God is for us and is helping us grow in ways that will produce eternal life.

CHAPTER 11

MERCY AND GRACE

MERCY AND GRACE ARE LIKE
ARMOR AGAINST SIN

Mercy and grace. What does it take to obtain these and what changes do they make inside of a life? These attributes of God are deeply embedded identities of His that are glorious beyond my simple understanding!

Simply put, mercy is why I am clean before God the Father. Grace will keep me that way.

When I was in Hell, I understood with supernatural revelation the parable Jesus taught us about unforgiveness (see Matt. 18). I understood that it was because of my lack of mercy that it was completely righteous for me to be sentenced to Hell.

The conversation begins with Jesus being asked who is the greatest in the Kingdom of Heaven. This is an important question. If we know who God says is the most important, then we can structure our lives in the same way as great ones to achieve that same greatness.

Jesus answered by bringing a little child in front of everyone as an object lesson. Then He said:

> *Assuredly, I say to you, unless you are converted and become as little children, you will by no means enter the kingdom of heaven. Therefore whoever humbles himself as this little child is the greatest in the kingdom of heaven. Whoever receives one little child like this in My name receives Me. But whoever causes one of these little ones who believe in Me to sin, it would be better for him if a millstone were hung around his neck, and he were drowned in the depth of the sea* (Matthew 18:3-6).

I have pondered His answer. Is He answering the question He was asked or giving the answer to a question that should have been asked? First, how "little" of a child did Jesus choose? Technically, a child in Jesus' time was someone under the age of 13 years old. At 13, boys were considered to be men. But who is a little child? Children had chores, but little children were, like today, not really given chores. Not much has changed between the little children of Jesus' day and ours.

For the sake of discussion, let's choose a boy child of five years old. This is a little less than half the age of maturity at Jesus' time. I have a grandson who is five years old. He is a delight! He needs help getting dressed, putting on his shoes, bathing, and cutting up his food as well as the security from his parents to be at peace. He is a little child. He also possesses innocence, obedience, affection, acceptance, and trust.

For Jesus to put the child in front of everyone messes with me, and I think it may have messed with them. The question, remember, is who is the *greatest* in the Kingdom of Heaven.

If you were to ask me who I think is the greatest, I may give answers like God, Moses, Abraham, David, etc. I am sure that object lesson was not what anyone would have expected. And how crazy to be told that they had to be *converted* and *become* like the object lesson or *they would never enter into the Kingdom of Heaven.*

These words were confusing to say the least, and who would want to go back to being a little child?

The dialogue continues as Jesus says that whoever is guilty of causing a child not to believe in Him is better off dead. And then He says:

> *Woe to the world because of offenses! For offenses must come, but woe to that man by whom the offense comes!* (Matthew 18:7)

Stop the story! I mean what is happening? Why is Jesus now speaking about offenses? And to use such a strong introduction as "Woe," which means great sorrow or distress. How powerful then is an offense?

Though it seems confusing, Jesus begins addressing the whole topic of offense because the object lesson *was* offensive. He was telling how to enter the Kingdom of Heaven and the hearers didn't want to accept His way.

Jesus continues talking to the people:

> *If your hand or foot causes you to sin, cut it off and cast it from you. It is better for you to enter into life lame or maimed, rather than having two hands or two feet, to be cast into the everlasting fire. And if your eye causes you to sin, pluck it out and cast it from you. It is better for you to enter into life with one eye, rather than having two eyes, to be cast into hell fire. Take heed that you do not despise one of these little ones, for I say to you that in heaven their angels always see the face of My Father who is in heaven* (Matthew 18:8-10).

I am a literal person. I do not have a problem with what Jesus said. I think Jesus is being very serious about sin and so should we. I understood in Hell that Jesus is helping us by telling us these seemingly harsh words. If I want to say that it is my hand that is causing me to sin, then I need to get rid of it so that I do not end up in Hell but rather can enter Heaven. Or if I am going to say that it is my eyes that are the reason I sin then I should blind myself so that I stop sinning and am not cast into Hell.

These seem like such extreme measures, which Jesus deemed necessary to enter the Kingdom of Heaven. And yet, if we are not careful we miss the extreme warning about offenses.

Jesus continues: *"For the Son of Man has come to save that which was lost"* (Matt. 18:11).

This is one of my favorite scriptures, which is often taken out of context. Jesus is still talking about people being offended. He goes on to tell the story of a shepherd who will leave the 99 sheep that are safe and go find the one that is lost. Then the man will celebrate because the lost one has been found. This was an example everyone could identify with because shepherding was a common job. Then He says:

> *Even so it is not the will of your Father who is in heaven that one of these little ones should perish* (Matthew 18:14).

Jesus is tying together the truths that He came to save the lost, that everyone should go find the lost one, and that the Father in Heaven doesn't want anyone to perish. According to the dictionary, *perish* means to die, especially in a violent or sudden way, to suffer complete ruin or destruction. He is helping us understand that the question of who is the greatest in the Kingdom of Heaven is not as simple as giving the name of someone we think is a good person. In fact, just getting to Heaven requires a great effort. We must pay attention, be diligent, and become like children in our trust and obedience to God.

As Jesus continues, He discusses the problems between people. Isn't this where the majority of offenses take place?

> *Moreover if your brother sins against you, go and tell him his fault between you and him alone. If he hears you, you have*

gained your brother. But if he will not hear, take with you one or two more, that "by the mouth of two or three witnesses every word may be established." And if he refuses to hear them, tell it to the church. But if he refuses even to hear the church, let him be to you like a heathen and a tax collector (Matthew 18:15-17).

Offenses, remember, are dangerous. Jesus is giving us directions that are very timely. Jesus spells out what to do in a simple four-step process so that offenses don't cause us to suffer.

Step 1

Go talk to the person. When someone sins against us, we should go talk to them. Truthfully, this is not something I want to do. I want the person to "*know*" that they have hurt me. I begin pulling away and making judgments in my heart about them. I start thinking that they did it on purpose and that they will keep doing it on purpose. My natural tendency, instead of doing step one in Jesus' plan, is to create a "but" as explained in the previous chapter.

When I have humbled myself and gone to talk to the person, it almost always reveals itself to have been a big misunderstanding, unclear communication, hyper sensitivity, or at the very least a lack of clarity. Most of the time there is no need for step two.

I have a sweet granddaughter who is very special to me. For her birthday she forgoes a special present to have a three-day sleepover. She is a "quality time" child. One year, we started day one of the sleepover only to discover that a distant relative would arrive in the morning as a surprise. Instead of being able to hang out and play, I had to get groceries and prepare for the visit. I explained that she could sleep over that one night but that she would need to go home in the morning and we would reschedule the sleepover.

What she heard with my explanation was that her sleepover wasn't important and that all she would get was a grocery shopping trip and a frantic time of preparation for company. She also believed she would have to wait for her next birthday to have another three-day sleepover.

She became very unruly, disrespectful, and all-around difficult, but I didn't realize why at the time. She requested to go home. Once home she explained her story to my daughter who called me right away. She knew there was a mix-up as it is our great delight to have our grandchildren stay with us.

I returned to speak with our granddaughter who was by now quite an emotional mess. (I believe many of us have learned how to hide the emotional mess as we have grown up.)

I began by telling her how sorry I was that there was a problem and I thanked her for trusting me to listen to her as she explained her side. She burst into tears as she tried to tell me how much she loves me and how much she had looked forward, since her last birthday, to get to spend three days with me. I let her get everything out. I have found that letting someone tell me everything before I talk is most important. (This takes practice.) I hugged her and explained that this was a misunderstanding. I explained that it wouldn't be the last misunderstanding in our lives, as they happen all the time to almost everyone. I explained again but this time I took more time and gave her more details. I also gave her dates to look forward to and offered for her to come back with me to sleep over that night as a bonus.

I took the blame, or at least 51 percent of it. I asked her to forgive me and she grabbed me and hugged me tightly. She told me that it was all her fault and asked me to forgive her. My granddaughter learned a very valuable lesson that day about following Jesus' plan for handling offense. She learned the importance of talking to someone who has caused hurt so she could get her heart clean.

Relationships are very fragile and Jesus gave the perfect plan for fixing problems. If step one doesn't work, we must continue to the end because offense is dangerous.

Step 2

Try again, but this time with a witness. Notice Jesus said a witness. This can be an eyewitness, a person who can establish that something is wrong or provide guidance as to the correct way, or a person who has firsthand knowledge about the problem and is committed to helping find a solution.

In my experience, there are fewer times we get to this step because usually the problem can be fixed at step one. However, I remember when my oldest daughter called and asked if we could have a girl's night out—just my two daughters and me. I was excited and said yes. They chose a Mexican restaurant and as soon as the order was placed, our oldest daughter said, "Mom we want to talk to you about how you are treating Dad. We feel that you are not listening to us individually so we want to bring it up together." I was instantly upset.

They both told me things they did not like. They took turns telling me all kinds of patterns they were noticing. Then they ended by telling me how much they loved me and wanted everything inside my marriage to their dad to be right. I was very defensive, argumentative, and unpleasant, to say the least.

We had also planned on a window-shopping time to follow dinner. When we arrived at the mall, I slipped away to pout. Our oldest daughter called me and asked where I was. Then she said, "Mom, you know we are right. You need to repent to Dad when you get home. You know he will forgive you. You need to come hang out with us because we won't get to do this again for a while."

It was like a light went on. Both our daughters had seen my behavior and God was sending them to help me. By the way, Mike did forgive me and all of our relationships are stronger because of it.

Step 3

Try again. This time involve the church. This means a trusted pastor, elders, or leader.

When I first got saved, we belonged to a church that had a prayer chain. A friend, who was also on our church board, was sick. I stopped by and she shared that she was facing a cancer threat and her appointment was later that day. I called someone on the prayer chain so the church could pray. The whole church was notified in only a few hours. Then, I received a phone call from the leader of the prayer chain requesting a meeting the next afternoon.

That same day, I went back to visit our friend after her doctor's appointment and learned more of her situation. I made a second call to let the prayer chain know how it had gone. Then I had a brilliant idea to call and put my sick friend on prayer chains of other churches. By nightfall, our whole town of prayer chains had been contacted. I was very proud of my efforts.

In a short time, my sick friend called to tell me how upset she was that I had shared about her sickness with the prayer chain at our church. For her it was very private and she had only told me as a personal friend. I was sorry and wondered if I should tell her that I had called other churches as well or if that would make it worse. I decided to tell her everything. She was very upset.

In the early evening, I received a call requesting that I meet with an elder of our church the next day. When I arrived, my sick friend, the lady in charge of the prayer chain, and the elder were waiting for me. It was very intimidating!

The elder asked me if I knew why I was there. He was very patient and kind. He asked me to explain about what I knew had happened about the prayer chain. When I finished, the prayer chain leader wanted to know why I had made the second call after she had set up a meeting with me. I explained how I didn't know she was meeting with me because I had done a wrong thing. I thought she was wanting to get to know me better.

The elder said that he believed I had told the truth. He said that he loved my heart but that my actions had resulted in gossip. It was all true information but it was all true gossip because if we share anyone's stuff without their permission, it is gossip. He asked me if I understood that I had hurt my friend. I could see it clearly now.

He explained that my friend had shared with me because she wanted me to pray. It was for her to put herself on the prayer chain. He also explained how only the prayer chain leader starts the chain and that everyone on the chain should be reminded of that fact. He clarified that contacting other churches is the job of the pastor or an elder. He told me that I was a leader and that he wanted to help me understand the ways of godly leadership.

He said, "Laurie, please forgive me for not having done a better job of explaining the ways of God to you." I was shocked. Wasn't I the one in trouble? The prayer chain leader asked for forgiveness for the team not responding correctly and it all getting out of hand.

My friend asked me to forgive her for becoming so offended. She said that prayer is a very good thing and because of her fear she had left out prayer. I couldn't believe that getting all the people involved with the church could have turned out so lovingly. But Jesus knew this all along.

Step 4

Treat him like a heathen or tax collector—neither of them know God.

Jesus is our perfect example. How did He treat someone who doesn't know God? Didn't He try to make sure that everyone would have an opportunity to know Him and His ways? Jesus brought both tax collectors and heathens to the saving knowledge of His Father because the Father desires that none should perish (see 2 Pet. 3:9). A person cannot be godly if they don't know God. So Jesus is warning us to beware of the heathen and tax collector and not trust them as we would a fellow believer. But we should help them to know our Father and to become like Him.

> *Assuredly, I say to you, whatever you bind on earth will be bound in heaven, and whatever you loose on earth will be loosed in heaven. Again I say to you that if two of you agree on earth concerning anything that they ask, it will be done for them by My Father in heaven. For where two or three are gathered together in My name, I am there in the midst of them* (Matthew 18:18-20).

There are many teachings about the binding and loosing meanings of this scripture. The first meaning of this, inside of its context, is referring to being reconciled to your brother and getting out of offense.

The chapter continues with Peter asking Jesus about how often he should forgive and how many times someone should be allowed to sin against him. Then Peter offers an answer of the number seven, believing he was being very generous in offering the perfect number. In Hell, I understood this question and answer very clearly.

> *Then Peter came to Jesus and asked, "Lord, how many times shall I forgive my brother or sister who sins against me? Up to seven times?" Jesus answered, "I tell you, not seven times, but seventy-seven times"* (Matthew 18:21-22 NIV).

Jesus is revealing His heart about forgiveness and offense. To further answer the question, Jesus gives Peter the famous parable of the unforgiving servant. In Hell, there were so many people there for unforgiveness and every one of us knew that this parable exemplified why we were guilty.

> *Therefore, the kingdom of heaven is like a king who wanted to settle accounts with his servants. As he began the settlement, a man who owed him ten thousand bags of gold was brought to him. Since he was not able to pay, the master ordered that*

he and his wife and his children and all that he had be sold to repay the debt.

At this the servant fell on his knees before him. "Be patient with me," he begged, "and I will pay back everything." The servant's master took pity on him, canceled the debt and let him go.

But when that servant went out, he found one of his fellow servants who owed him a hundred silver coins. He grabbed him and began to choke him. "Pay back what you owe me!" he demanded. His fellow servant fell to his knees and begged him, "Be patient with me, and I will pay it back." But he refused. Instead, he went off and had the man thrown into prison until he could pay the debt. When the other servants saw what had happened, they were outraged and went and told their master everything that had happened.

Then the master called the servant in. "You wicked servant," he said, "I canceled all that debt of yours because you begged me to. Shouldn't you have had mercy on your fellow servant just as I had on you?" In anger his master handed him over to the jailers to be tortured, until he should pay back all he owed (Matthew 18:23-34 NIV).

Throughout Matthew 18 Jesus ties together and warns us with these truths:

- Understanding how to be the greatest in the Kingdom of Heaven;
- Becoming like and being converted as little children in order to enter the Kingdom of Heaven;
- Cutting off a foot that causes sin;

- Knowing that the Son of Man came to save that which was lost;

- Believing the fact that it is not the will of the Father that one of these little ones should perish;

- Going to our brother if he sins against us in a four-step plan;

- Answering the question of how many times we should forgive our brother;

- But especially in His warning:

So My heavenly Father also will do to you if each of you, from his heart, does not forgive his brother his trespasses (Matthew 18:35).

I was in Hell, eternally, because I would not forgive others.

Since Hell, I have studied the parable of the unforgiving servant and will probably always study it. I believe that it is key to understanding the necessity of mercy and grace.

The king in the parable is like the King in Heaven. Jesus shares the ways of the king, which implies that this story is a trustworthy example of the ways of Heaven.

The King of Heaven, like the king of the parable, will settle accounts. We will stand before the King in the same way that the servant in the parable did and give account for what we owe. This servant owed 10,000 talents. In the economy of the time, this would be about 200,000 years' wages.

So, 10,000 talents are easily described as a debt that could *never* be repaid. And when the servant asked the King to have patience with him, it was a ridiculous request. This servant could never pay it back. Instead of patience, the King offered something else—mercy and grace.

Mercy and grace are often confused. While the terms have similar meanings, grace and mercy are not the same. To summarize the difference:

Mercy is God not punishing us as our sins deserve, and grace is God blessing us despite the fact that we do not deserve it. Mercy is deliverance from judgment. Grace is extending kindness to the unworthy.[1]

When the servant sees the King again the situation is dire.

> *"You wicked servant,"* he said, *"I canceled all that debt of yours because you begged me to. Shouldn't you have had mercy on your fellow servant just as I had on you?"* In anger his master handed him over to the jailers to be tortured, until he should pay back all he owed (Matthew 18:32-34 NIV).

What Jesus is teaching in the parable is that when He forgives the debt, He is also giving pieces of His identity, which are mercy and grace. The wicked servant of this parable only accepted the debt cancellation and not the identity of becoming merciful and filled with grace.

The wicked servant asked for patience, for time to pay back the debt. The king could have done as he asked and given an extension of the due date or he could have cut the debt in half. Instead, what the king gave His servant was a very kingly identity gift that should have changed him. There should have been a heart transformation. But the servant only received the cancelled debt, not the gifts of mercy and grace that would have transformed him.

Similarly, when Jesus forgave my sins, if I actually received that gift from Him, I also received the ability to become merciful like Him. If all I received was just the cancelled debt and not the heart of mercy that was extended, then all I can do is choose to cancel a debt when someone wrongs me. I don't have the ability to extend mercy and grace until I can receive it (see 2 Cor. 1:4).

When the servant missed the heart of the king, he placed himself outside the mercy and grace of the king. If I cannot receive the gift from the king, I am not really in relationship with Him. I have an inability to be like Him.

This parable is important because, at first glance, it appears that a rich king simply looked the other way about a debt because it wasn't important. When we study it, we see that the hard-hearted servant wouldn't change even after the king gave him the greatest gift he could have received. Therefore, the wicked servant doesn't want to be part of that kingdom.

It leaves the king in the parable angry. Similarly, it makes our King angry when we won't receive the gift He has given us. The man took it, but he didn't let the gift change him.

So when Jesus says, "My heavenly Father will do the same to you if you don't forgive from your heart," it has nothing to do with debt and everything to do with mercy and grace. If I really did receive mercy from Jesus, then that gift of being forgiven should change me and I should not only desire to forgive but be able and willing.

Like the servant, Jesus has forgiven me a debt too large for me to ever repay. The cost for my sin is innocent shed blood. The only one who has ever had that price to pay for any sin is Jesus Christ, the pure spotless Lamb! When He forgave me, it was more than just paying for my sin. In truly receiving His gift of mercy and grace for my sins, my heart should have become one that owns and uses His powerful gifts.

In the parable, the problem is not that the servant didn't release the fellow servant from the debt of money. He may have needed the money to be paid back. The problem was that he had not received the gift and heart transformation of mercy from the king to be like the king and had only received the cancelling of the monetary debt. The king gave him more than a debt cancellation.

Then the wicked servant had the other servant thrown into prison where he could never make money to pay his debt. Therefore, the wicked servant was punished by the king for his actions against his fellow servant.

This made the king very angry. He desires that his ways be replicated in his kingdom.

Now let's look at the heavenly Father's gift of mercy to me. I am a sinner. My sin will take me to Hell. No amount of patience will fix my sin. The only fix is innocent shed blood, and only Jesus, the Son of God, has any. The payment includes His suffering the most terrible of deaths on the cross to procure it.

I was forgiven every sin so that I can be allowed to enter into the Kingdom of Heaven. Receiving this gift into my heart included receiving God and His ways of mercy and grace. I have to choose to not only have patience but to also be like my Savior and extend mercy and grace to my offenders.

When I went to Hell, I went because I would not forgive. I would not follow Jesus' great example.

Pray the Lord's Prayer with me:

> *Our Father which art in heaven, Hallowed be thy name. Thy kingdom come, Thy will be done in earth, as it is in heaven. Give us this day our daily bread. And forgive us our debts, as we forgive our debtors. And lead us not into temptation, but deliver us from evil: For thine is the kingdom, and the power, and the glory, for ever. Amen* (Matthew 6:9-13 KJV).

Unforgiveness is very dangerous! In the words of Jesus' warning, "*So My heavenly Father also will do to you if each of you, from his heart, does not forgive his brother his trespasses*" (Matt. 18:35).

NOTE

1. "What is the difference between mercy and grace?" Gotquestions.org, accessed October 3, 2018, https://www.gotquestions.org/mercy-grace .html.

CHAPTER 12

WATCHFULNESS

I am still learning from my experience in Hell. I read the Scriptures and have a new appreciation and understanding of them every day. I say this not to convince you to believe my personal revelations but rather to encourage you to take the topic of eternity seriously and seek out the Scriptures yourself. After we die, we will each spend forever someplace. Be warned, there are only two places, Heaven and Hell, and the choice is *ours*.

I have heard it said, "A minute after you die you will know exactly how you *should* have lived." I don't believe it takes a whole minute. The reality is that Jesus came to help us know about eternity and how we should live *before* we die so that we will not be shocked in the seconds after we die.

As a messenger, I talk to people all the time who truly believe they are going to Heaven on the basis that they feel they are good people. They explain that they don't sin any more than the next guy. They also believe that the idea of having to live "perfect" is ridiculous and impossible. They continue that the God they believe in will certainly let them into Heaven based on the assurance of *His* goodness.

When I ask about their life plan to *try* to become sinless they get angry, make a joke, or get saved. People in general don't like to be told what to do.

We don't like to be told that what we are doing in our own strength isn't enough or that it doesn't measure up. However, unless we engage people with the truth about sin and they repent, they are not truly saved.

In Hell, I was "watchful." As I said before, I knew some worse thing was getting ready to happen. Even though we were already in a lot of pain, I knew that something *much* worse was coming and it was terrifying. It was unfathomable and inevitable.

My watchfulness in Hell was in direct contrast to my lackadaisical attitude beforehand. Today, I am very seriously watchful with an extreme soberness. I believe we all should be! Many people are going to go to Hell. Many who call Jesus "Lord, Lord" are going to Hell. They are not ready!

I am ridiculed about this more than any part of the Hell experience. I am belittled, challenged, and rebuked for telling how we must stop sinning! I have been called a perfectionist, a Pharisee, a legalist, a manipulator, a charlatan, a liar, a fake, a quack, and a deceiver all because I believe in, preach, teach, desire, ascribe to, and demand holiness in myself and others.

The Bible says:

> *You therefore must be perfect, as your heavenly Father is perfect* (Matthew 5:48 ESV).

> *For it is written, "You must be holy, because I am holy"* (1 Peter 1:16 ISV).

What is the big deal with holiness? In holiness we find communion with God. If sin separates us from Him, then sinlessness keeps us close. I understand about the assurance of salvation and the mighty work of sanctification and how God has abundantly more patience than I do. *But,* I find that there is such a deception about holiness—as if it is an unattainable and ungodly expectation and, therefore, a bad word.

There is a story about Jesus and a woman who was caught in adultery. She is brought and thrown at His feet. All the religious people around the situation want her stoned. The story continues that Jesus writes something in the dirt and then gives the okay for her to be stoned with the requirement that the first stone must be thrown by the person who is sinless. No one threw a stone and one by one they left from the oldest to the youngest. Meaning they were *all* guilty of sin.

Then Jesus asks the woman if no one is going to accuse her. And He says that He will not accuse her either. Then He tells her to do something. He tells her to go *and* sin no more.

I was a student at the Reinhard Bonnke School of Evangelism. He told us that the Lord had shared with him what Jesus wrote in the dirt. Reinhard said it was one word—*guilty*.

I have thought about it myself and I believe that God did speak to Reinhard. Who isn't guilty? The only person who could have cast the first stone was Jesus, and He chose not to. However, He did not condone sin or coddle the woman or tell her that He understood that holiness is just too hard. Instead, He gave her a simple instruction to stop sinning. In other words, be holy.

I am sure, after her life was just handed back her, that she didn't respond that it was just too hard. If Jesus says do it, it is because it can be done in the grace that He will give to accomplish the thing He commanded. Everything else is disobedience. Beware, disobedience can be very deceptive, with shocking outcomes. Think of Adam and Eve.

The Bible says:

> *For the wages of sin is death, but the free gift of God is eternal life in Christ Jesus our Lord* (Romans 6:23 ESV).

> *Everyone who makes a practice of sinning also practices lawlessness; sin is lawlessness* (1 John 3:4 ESV).

> *Whoever believes in the Son has eternal life; whoever does not obey the Son shall not see life, but the wrath of God remains on him* (John 3:36 ESV).

For if we go on sinning deliberately after receiving the knowledge of the truth, there no longer remains a sacrifice for sins (Hebrews 10:26 ESV).

The fear of the Lord is hatred of evil (Proverbs 8:13 ESV).

Sin and eternal life do not mix.

The watchfulness I possess since coming back from Hell is in four areas.

1. My life

2. The lives of my family, friends, and church

3. The lost

4. The times

WATCHFULNESS IN OUR LIVES

The Bible has many scriptures that should put the fear of the Lord in us; here is one:

Not everyone who says to Me, "Lord, Lord," shall enter the kingdom of heaven, but he who does the will of My Father in heaven. Many will say to Me in that day, "Lord, Lord, have we not prophesied in Your name, cast out demons in Your name, and done many wonders [miracles] in Your name?" And then I will declare to them, "I never knew you; depart from Me, you who practice lawlessness!" (Matthew 7:21-23)

Who are these people? They tell others the word of the Lord, cast out unclean spirits, and do miracles all in the name of Jesus.

Yet Jesus tells them that they will not be allowed into Heaven with Him because they practice lawlessness. The dictionary says lawlessness is a state in which there is widespread wrongdoing and disregard for rules and authority. In this case, disregard for God's rules and His authority.

This scripture should cause us to be watchful! I remember the first time I read this passage and it put the fear of the Lord in me! I prayed afterward to Jesus for His help to identify these people, especially if it was me.

And it was me! I was in Hell because I would not forgive—a direct act of lawlessness. I would have never believed that I was going to Hell for not forgiving. I prayed, heard God for others, tithed, fasted, served on deliverance teams, and believed in and saw miracles. Yet I was blind to my own lawlessness. In Hell, I knew I was the person Jesus is talking about in this scripture, the one He never knew.

Jesus also tells a parable of ten virgins, which teaches what it takes to make it to Heaven. He begins by putting it in the context of a wedding. In Jesus' time, a virgin waited for her bridegroom to come in the night. She had to be ready when he came.

Jesus tells us that there were five wise and five foolish virgins waiting for the one they loved. The wise had oil for their lamps. A bride in that time had to have oil for her lamp or she could not light her way to go with the bridegroom. It was an essential item. Much like a ring or a dress would be in today's ceremonies. Five wise virgins had oil and were ready to be married. The five foolish did not have oil. They were not prepared in their heart to be married.

At midnight they all learned that the bridegroom was coming. The foolish virgins were not ready so they asked the wise virgins to give them some oil. This was ridiculous! No one would wait until their wedding day to find, purchase, and size a wedding gown or ring. Nor would a woman give away her dress or ring to another on her own wedding day. It was an impossible request that the foolish virgins shouldn't have even made.

When the bridegroom arrived, the wise virgins joined him and the ceremony continued as planned. Later, the foolish virgins came to the bridegroom asking be included. But the bridegroom answered them by saying that he did not know them (see Matt. 25:1-12).

And then Jesus made the most serious statement when He said, "*Watch therefore, for you know neither the day nor the hour in which the Son of Man is coming*" (Matthew 25:13).

Who are these people Jesus warns to "watch therefore"? What is the oil of which He speaks? This parable is for all people who are waiting for the Son of Man, Jesus. The oil represents their relationship with Him. They are warned to be ready.

I was like a foolish virgin. I was not watchful or ready. I went to Hell because I would not forgive, because I did not walk in obedience or stay under His authority. Instead, I took upon myself lawlessness in choosing whom I would forgive.

The truth is, I was not in communion with Him. I was in sin, which separated me from God. In Hell, I was forgotten. When God tore His garment across His heart, I knew that I was like the foolish virgins—left out.

This scripture was clear in Hell! It is all about some people coming into the everlasting presence of life with God and some people being cast out into outer darkness and everlasting punishment.

My watchfulness has increased because I take my everlasting eternity very seriously! I have added to my life of prayer, "Lord did I do what You needed me to do today? Am I guilty of sin today?" He is always faithful to tell me when I am in sin. If I forget to pray, I have given Him permission to bring me the truth of the condition of my soul. I now expect a dream, to hear from a friend, or any means He needs to use because it is my desire to be holy!

WATCHFULNESS FOR OTHERS

I am watchful for my family, friends, and the people of God's Church. And I desire for them to be watchful over me. In Hell, I understood so clearly the statement, "Am I my brother's keeper?"

We see in Genesis 4 the story of Cain and Abel. They are each bringing a sacrifice to God. It appears that Abel, a sheep farmer, is bringing a sheep and Cain, a vegetable farmer, is bringing some veggies. God accepts the sheep but will not accept the vegetables. This makes Cain angry. God tells Cain to bring Him the correct sacrifice and He will accept it. God warns Cain that sin is waiting for him but that Cain should rule over it. What Cain does next is shocking. He goes and talks with his brother Abel and then murders him.

God asks Cain *"Where is Abel your brother?"* and Cain answers, *"I do not know. Am I my brother's keeper?"* (Gen. 4:9).

I remember the first time I read this and how confused I was. Who gets mad at God and then murders his family? And if God knows everything in advance, how come He wouldn't accept the vegetables?

Let me stop here to remind us of a very important rule about reading Scripture. If ever we read the Bible and think that God is the bad guy, we are 100 percent wrong. God can never be the bad guy, ever. When this happens, stop and pray and ask the Holy Spirit for His help or go get help because misunderstanding the Bible will cause us to lose trust in the Lord.

In the beginning of time, when Adam and Eve sinned, a standard for atonement and making things right by sacrifice was set by God. The *only* acceptable sacrifice was and is the innocent blood of a slain lamb. It had not changed just because Abel was a sheep farmer. He had to offer the blood of one of the lambs he loved to cover his sin. Not only did Abel have to give a lamb for the sacrifice for his sin but also for the others who needed a sacrifice as well. So even more of the sheep that he loved would be slain.

It had not changed because Cain was a vegetable farmer. What Cain brought instead of the lamb was his pride. He had produced vegetables in the ground that God said would produce thorns and thistles. Cain decided that God should change the set atonement. When God would not, Cain still changed the necessary offering. Instead of the innocent blood of a lamb, he shed the blood of the innocent shepherd of the sheep. Not just the shepherd but his innocent brother. Cain's pride not only stopped his heart from obeying God but it also removed the brotherly love and replaced it with hate. So when he answered God with, "Am I my brother's keeper?" his answer was filled with hate.

I understood in Hell how intricately we are connected to one another. The answer to "am I my brother's keeper" is *yes*, with a few minor acknowledgements. When we look at the heart of Cain, we do not see a person willing to obey God. If we are not willing to obey God, we will not have anyone else's best interests before ours.

Although every person is responsible for his or her own actions before God, our interactions with one another make us accountable before God in another person's life. Charles Spurgeon has an excellent sermon on the topic of being our brother's keeper where he breaks down how we cannot secure salvation for anyone other than ourselves. This includes promises over infants to be perfect or prayers over individuals declaring their salvation outside of a repentant response from the individual.

However, as a Christian person we have power from Jesus to do good for others and that includes the responsibility to introduce others to Him. Jesus taught us to love our neighbor as we love ourselves (see Mark 12:30-31). To do this, we must love our neighbor's soul. Loving a soul does not mean we have to love the person's actions, personality, or current identity. Rather, we should love the God-given soul in that person that He desires to have with Him eternally.

Once I was on an outreach and began talking to a man who was sitting on a cement wall. I explained that we were out praying for people, and he thanked me for my work for the Kingdom. I asked him if he was a believer and he said that he was. I kept asking God for insight because something seemed off. He said that he believed and followed God, then he added a little quietly, "Well, in almost everything." I asked if he could share in what way he wasn't following God.

He told me that first I needed to understand that no believer is expected to put up with or allow the things that had happened to him. He said that he hated his son and that he hopes his son will rot in Hell.

He got very agitated and told me that his son was so disrespectful to him, used him, owed him money, and lied to him. I told him that it sounds just like a teenage boy. I offered that he must not have grown out of it but that is what we parents deal with. But the man wasn't budging in his hatred toward his son.

I told him that even non-Christian families don't want their children in Hell for their bad behavior. So he explained. The incident that ended their relationship happened over 20 years before, when the son was 19 years old. Afterward, he had kicked his son out of his home and life and had not received his son's attempts to reconcile. He even had grandchildren he had never met and he felt they needed to follow their father to Hell.

I didn't like this man or his ways. I didn't want his terrible thoughts around me. Then something remarkable happened. It changed from just a chit-chat to a matter of what I call "soul love." I stepped close to the man and placed my hands on his face, which helped illustrate the desperateness of his situation.

I explained, "Brother, you have it all wrong and unless you repent, *you* will not see God." He glared at me as tears filled my eyes. "How has Satan turned your heart to bitter stone against the gift the Lord has given you? Repent, please...repent."

While I had my hands cupped on his face, his wife walked up and said, "Excuse me, that is *my* husband!"

I turned to her, without removing my hands, and calmly said, "I am helping him forgive your son before it is too late for his soul." Right then and there she started praying. She asked me to continue.

Long story short, the man was angry that I had challenged him. He was very upset to find out that God was not on his side about his son and grandchildren going to Hell. He was furious when I told him that he has no heavenly right to deny his wife permission to see their son and their grandchildren. He was beyond mad when I said that unless he repents, he will not enter the Kingdom of Heaven.

He said that he would rather go to Hell than forgive! I responded in the softest voice, now holding his hands, "Satan, you stop talking to this man while I am here, in the name of Jesus!" The man had a distant look in his eyes.

Then I asked him this question: "Has Satan ever used your son's life to hurt you?" He nodded. I continued, "Has Satan ever used your life to hurt anyone?" He looked at me and I could see tears forming in his eyes.

I told him, "You and your son are alike. But you are in more danger than your son because you refuse to obey God." His eyes turned from the soft place to so much hatred. He told me to move. As he was leaving he said that both he, his boy, and the children could rot in Hell for all he cared.

I was struggling to process his hatred toward his son. How much hatred is in a person to will themselves into Hell? But I ran to catch up to him. He stopped and I said, "You are still a son of God; do not let Satan cause you to walk away from your Savior. Repent and be reconciled, in the name of Jesus."

He stood there shaking his head no while I kept nodding mine yes. Then he nodded. I have no idea what it meant. I can't tell you what his no symbolized or what my yes insinuated. But I knew when he nodded yes, something was better.

His wife hugged me. She said that no one has ever talked to him like I had, filled with love and correction. She wished that the pastor would have done it years ago. She asked me what she should do. I told her to keep praying and to keep loving her husband's soul. Soul love is very powerful! It is the example Jesus gave us, and it didn't fail Him. The Bible says, "If you can't love your brother who you can see, how can you love God who you cannot see?" (see 1 John 4:20).

Even more, Jesus goes so far as to ask us to love our enemy. The Bible says that Jesus becoming a man is proof that He loved us while we were still His enemies (see Rom. 5:10). This whole concept puts me on a tilt every time I try to understand it. The plan to save mankind is to send God Himself.

Here is how I explain it to people who think it is all too hard to understand. I begin with asking a question: "Would you ever become, forever, a goldfish to talk and relate to other fish so that they would know you love them?" I hear all kinds of answers as to why not. Even little children know they do not want to be a little fish. It seems ridiculous doesn't it?

Yet God became a man to talk with and relate to us so that we would know He loves us. He became His brother's keeper. And He chose to come as a baby. You can't get more vulnerable than that. Incredible! It was because we all need Him, the Savior of the world. Everyone is trapped by sin.

According to the ways of God, the needy people of the world have a claim on the people of God (see Matt. 25:35). We are the salt and light of the world. As Christians, we are commanded to help others, making me my brother's keeper. To do this we will need the help of God the Holy Spirit. What greater need does anyone have than the knowledge of God?

God put us in the time period we live in, in a certain geographical area and in a specific family, to accomplish a list of very important works for Him. One of which is to tell others of Him. But what if we deny them the gospel? Will we hear "well done good and faithful servant" and be allowed to enter into the Kingdom He has prepared for us?

Save others by snatching them out of the fire; to others show mercy with fear, hating even the garment stained by the flesh (Jude 1:23 ESV).

The lost are all around us. Some have never known Jesus, while others have been in church their whole lives.

I watch for the lost ones. I meet them all the time, everywhere, in all walks of life. One time I was on a night outreach in October to a haunted house called the Edge of Hell. We took groups there to talk to the people waiting to go in or while they walked back to their cars.

On this particular night, I stopped a girl who looked extremely sad. She was young, maybe eight or ten years old. I asked her if she was with family and she said yes. I asked her to take me to them. I explained that it is not a safe area for a little girl to be walking around. Her family was close but not watching her. When I met her mom she was sitting up against a building with two other daughters. The woman was smoking and they all looked extremely sad.

I asked what had happened and the mom asked me if I was a believer in Jesus Christ. I was pleasantly surprised and answered that yes, I am a serious one. It was the right answer. They all started telling me about what a horrible week they had. The mom explained how her mother, the girl's grandmother, had died just the day before.

I told them I was so sorry. The girls were now crying. The grandmother had asked her daughter to bring the granddaughters over to see her but she had not. She said that since her mom was a Christian and she knew she was dying of cancer, the only thing she wanted was for them all to give their lives to Jesus. But the woman did not want her mother to pressure her. She had spoken to her mother the night before she died. The mother told her that if she did not give her life to Jesus Christ before she died, she would go to Hell. The daughter had argued that she was only saying that because she had not married the three different men who fathered her children. The conversation so upset her daughter that she had told her mom she never wanted to see her again. Her mother died the next day.

I asked the girls to tell me about their grandmother. They told me beautiful things like she spent all her money on them, took them with her on outings, took them to church and prayed for them all the time. They said how she was always peaceful and believed that it was a gift from Jesus to her. They said that their grandmother was the best in the world and that she loved them all very much.

The mom cried as she listened to the girls explain who their grand-mother was to them. I asked the woman who her mother was to her. She said her mom, the grandmother, was all the time correcting her, was very hard on her, and that she was always telling her she needed Jesus as if she was such a terrible sinner.

As I prayed I felt that I knew what I should say. So I told her that a dis-obedient child never feels loved. They think that the whole world hates them when in reality only their own disobedience makes them think the world hates them. I said that it is like wearing a pair of sound-stopping ear plugs—because you can't hear anything, you think no one is speaking to you. We all know when we are disobedient. We are our own worst company and nothing we do can compensate for the wrong things we have done.

I told them all that their mother and grandmother was right about the peace that only Jesus brings. I asked them why they were at the *Edge of Hell*. The mother said that the grandmother's words wouldn't let her be at peace. She decided that if there was a way to find peace at the *Edge of Hell*, she would do what her mother recommended even though it seemed too late. This family was at the event looking for Jesus. Grandmother had told them that in the darkest of places He is there.

I am in awe of our God who finds us and keeps us.

All four of them received Jesus. It was very powerful. First, the girls all repented out loud and most had the same issues. They asked Jesus to be the Lord of their lives. I asked them to forgive their mom and grandmother for always being upset with each other. They each prayed. I asked them how they felt and they all felt—*safe*. (Come on Jesus!)

I asked them if I could speak with their mom alone. I asked them to wait against the wall as I was not going to have them walk around in that unsafe area. I spoke bluntly with their mother. She agreed and could rec-ognize all of her disobedience toward Jesus. She asked Him to forgive so many individual things. Then I asked her to talk to the Lord about her relationship with her mom.

Her words were unrecognizable. The tears and wailing that came out of her caused her daughters to come over to be sure their mom was okay. I smiled and asked them to let her finish. They walked back to the wall hesitantly.

I said to the woman, "Tell Jesus that your mother has always loved you and pointed you in the right direction. Tell Him how you have lied to yourself and others about her, making her out to be a monster when really she was the best mom ever."

The woman started throwing up. Yep, I wasn't prepared for that!

When she finally stood up she looked like a different lady. She said she felt something very angry leave her. I took them all out for a celebration at a nearby fast-food restaurant. We talked about going to church the next morning, joining, and getting water baptized. Before we departed, we prayed for the baptism of the Holy Spirit.

We have no idea how hard God is working if we would only be watchful for the opportunities He puts right in front of us.

WATCHFULNESS OF THE TIMES

The spiritual clock is moving. The Bible says that no one knows the exact hour that Jesus is coming back except for the Father (see Mark 13:32). The Father will not be late. He knows exactly when Jesus needs to come and He is diligently watching the time.

Jesus told us many things that would let us know when the time is getting close, much like a woman in labor (see Rev. 12:2). He told us that in the "be ready" time, it would be like in the times of Noah (see Matt. 24:37-39). That there would be so much evil on the land.

There is more evil in the land now than there ever was in my lifetime or that of my grandparents. I believe that we are running out of time and the only right answer is to study the Bible and be ready, be watchful.

Watch, stand fast in the faith, be brave, be strong (1 Corinthians 16:13).

CHAPTER 13

HELL CONSPIRACY DEFINED

The Hell Conspiracy is affecting us all!

Simply put, Satan desires to hurt God by taking us, the objects of His affection, and causing us to reject God by any means possible so that we will be eternally separated from God in Hell.

Satan has weaved doubt and despair along with exalted pride to blind people of this Hell Conspiracy. And he is doing it in broad daylight, right under our noses. He convinces those lacking discernment to demand specific outcomes as proof of God's existence and to garner our continued loyalty to Jesus.

Not only this, but Satan has enraged the ignorant to shake angry fists at God. He has caused them to hate God, erase Him from their conscience for being God and declaring unmovable truths. Satan convinces the obstinate to declare unproven theories such as evolution as a scientific truth for esteeming man; to contend that murdering babies even when they could live outside the womb is a choice that is acceptable and good; and to accept the absurdity that the gender of a man or woman cannot and should not be determined at birth.

If this plan doesn't confuse the objects of God's affection, then the perpetual onslaught of sins including *"adultery, fornication, uncleanness, lewdness, idolatry, sorcery, hatred, contentions, jealousies, outbursts of wrath, selfish ambitions, dissensions, heresies, envy, murders, drunkenness, revelries, and the like"* (Gal. 5:19-21) which are practiced as acceptable will utterly confound them. Satan has convinced them that because times are changing, so will God. Forgetting the warning provided to us ahead of time, no one who practices these things will go to Heaven.

Satan has created such a complex and complicated web of confusing one-liners. Such statements as:

- "If God is real and is good, how could He let anyone go to eternal torment?"

- "If Jesus is mighty to save how could anyone perish?!"

- "Hell is preached to manipulate and control as a scare tactic when the Bible teaches us not to fear."

- "Everyone is ornately good and deserving of heaven!"

- "Don't worry, I try to be good."

All these lead to the absolute worse conspiracy of all—the false grace message. This deceit has created an entirely different facet to the Hell Conspiracy. I believe this deception will usher in the great falling away of which the Bible warns us. This facet of the Hell Conspiracy allows those who know God to believe that they may live their lives in sin and rebellion and that the prayer they prayed when they first repented allows their current sin to go unchecked and even allowed. In other words, once saved always saved.

Victoriously there is a voice that cuts through all the confusion. A voice that Satan cannot control, silence or stop. The Creator of Hell, The

Lord God Almighty, can dismantle the Hell Conspiracy quickly and completely if only we would choose to trust and obey. God did not create Hell for mankind and He is diligent and faithful to rescue all who cry out in wholeheartedness with an obedient soul. Repent and be saved!

CHAPTER 14

DETANGLING FROM THE HELL CONSPIRACY

REPENT AND BE SAVED

No one is good enough to get into Heaven on their own merit. Everyone must repent to be saved and repent to stay saved.

Salvation by Jesus alone is what allows us to go to Heaven. Salvation is a free gift from Jesus, but it is the most costly experience you will ever have. It is the great exchange. You will allow Jesus, an innocent Man, to take your place in Hell and pay the price for your sin. When you do this, you are agreeing to be purchased with His innocent blood, become His slave, and live your life wholeheartedly submitted to Him.

In exchange, you will not be counted guilty of your sins. Jesus will accept you with an unprecedented and unmeasurable amount of love and devotion. He will place your life in circumstances that will allow you to become more like Him through perseverance and trial. He will never leave you nor forsake you. You will find that although you come to Him as a slave, through that revelation, you find that He has made Himself your Father by the spirit of adoption. Additionally, He has made Himself your Brother, and even more, your Husband. As you continue, you will find that He is preparing you to rule and reign with Him.

Salvation begins with these truths.

- Believe that Jesus is the only Son of God, and He is God;

- Agree to surrender your entire life only to Him in total obedience;

- Repent of your sins.

Repentance is four things. If you don't do all four, you have not repented.

1. **Acknowledge sin:** Only God defines sin. Agree with His definition and acknowledge sin as sin. Agree that sin is deadly in your life.

2. **Godly sorrow:** This is not being "sorry." Godly sorrow might be best described as agonizing grief with inconsolable distress. This godly sorrow cannot be healed unless repentance is completed.

3. **Confess it and fix it:** Confess that you are in sin to a leader in your life. Together decide on how to best fix it. Fixing it means that you must rectify the wrong that the sin incurred. Fixing it will cost you.

4. **Build a stopper:** Put something in place to make sure you do not sin that way again. Sometimes we will repeat the same sin. This is grievous but with Jesus' help, you will overcome! Repeat steps one through three and realize that

a new step four is needed in addition to what you already have in place to actually overcome that sin.

HOW TO BEGIN

Once you realize that you need to detangle your life from the Hell Conspiracy you can receive Jesus as your Savior and let His ways bring clarity and holiness into your life.

Let's Pray:

Jesus, I need you. I realize that I am on my way to Hell. I deserve it. I know You love me and have made a way for me. I need Your way and Your rescue. Jesus would You take me as Yours? (Listen in your heart.)

Lord, these are my sins that I am guilty of: (Tell Jesus your sin, and why you did it.)

These sins and others like them take people to Hell and will take me to Hell unless I repent. Lord I choose to repent of them. Jesus send me to the place and people you have to help me grow, understand, and walk free of sin.

I love you Jesus. Thank You!

HELPFUL ACTS

There are other important acts that you need to do as a believer in Jesus Christ. Water Baptism, Baptism of the Holy Spirit and Communion are three:

Water baptism is very important! The Bible teaches that Jesus was baptized, He commanded you to be baptized, and the apostles also practiced water baptism. These truths are enough for you to be water baptized.

However, I recommend you take a water baptism class that can instruct you in a fuller understanding of this important step.

The Bible says when you are baptized, you are buried with Jesus Christ into His death and you now walk in His resurrection power. It may take you a lifetime to fully understand this, but the power of this obedience will begin to affect your life immediately. The spiritual leaders in your life can help you achieve this commandment.

Baptism of the Holy Spirit is essential to walk out a successful Christian life! When Jesus left the earth for Heaven, He did not leave you alone. He said before He left that He would send the Holy Spirit for you. The Holy Spirit is God! When you receive the baptism of the Holy Spirit, you receive Him into your life to direct and guide you. This powerful agreement with God includes many gifts like reading the Bible and understanding it, fitting in at church, speaking in tongues, trusting God, and obedience, just to name a few. The spiritual leaders in your life should be able to help you receive the Holy Spirit.

Communion is a powerful "reconnect" to God. On the night before Jesus died He told His disciples to do something in remembrance of Him. He took the Passover elements of wine and bread and gave them to His disciples in a powerful exchange.

Jesus told them to eat the bread because it was His body. Then He took a cup of wine and told them to drink it because it was His blood. He told them this was a new covenant for the forgiveness of their sins and those of many others.

This powerful conversion is for your daily life, especially when you find yourself in sin. When you sin, you cannot go back and say you need salvation as if you didn't already know Him. Similarly, you cannot say you need to be baptized again as if you were not already buried with Christ when you were baptized. You can't go back and undo a sin that the Holy Spirit was directing you not to do. You can, however, after repentance, enter into the reality of communion! When you do this, you remember what Jesus has done for you for the remission of your sins.

Jesus said that the person who has been forgiven much will love much. Remember what Jesus has done and partake of the communion bread and wine to enter into a powerful exchange of assurance, cleansing, and freedom today!

PART 4

HEAVENLY VISION OF THE CROSS

CHAPTER 15

THE CROSS

THE CROSS AND CUP OF WRATH

Since returning from Hell, my husband, Mike, and I study the cross. In the beginning it was the only place I found any comfort. I could not doubt the love of God once I studied the cross. I am thankful that this is where the Lord brought me because I have found comfort from my experiences in Hell at the foot of His cross.

When Mike and I travel to share my testimonies of Heaven and Hell, Mike gives a biblical blueprint for the realities of those two places. One of the truths we share is on Christ and the "Cup of Wrath." The truth we share is the person of Jesus Christ.

No other event in history ever displayed the glory of God's love so magnificently as the day the Lamb of God gave His life on the cross!

God made him who had no sin to be sin for us (2 Corinthians 5:21 NIV).

He was pierced for our transgressions; he was crushed for our iniquities (Isaiah 53:5 NIV).

It is my sin Jesus bears. He was punished in my place. My sins ripped His skin off, pressed thorns into His head, drove spikes into His hands and feet! I need to grasp how horrible and destructive sin is to us. I must gaze on the Lamb of God who took my sin upon Himself as the greatest act of love ever!

Let's start at the Garden of Gethsemane. The word *Gethsemane* means "crushed olives or oil press." It is a crushing place. It is here that the crushing and terrifying horror that Jesus went through began.

To understand, let's look at all of this through the topic of the anguish of the cup in the garden.

> *He had offered up prayers and supplications, with vehement cries and tears* (Hebrews 5:7).
>
> *My soul is exceedingly sorrowful, even to death* (Matthew 26:38).
>
> *And being in agony, He prayed more earnestly. Then His sweat became like great drops of blood falling down to the ground* (Luke 22:44).

Before the first whip mark touched His skin we see the Lord being pressed and blood being shed through His skin in unthinkable anguish. This is not a metaphor. There is a very rare phenomenon called *hematidrosis*, also known as bloody sweat. Under great emotional stress, the tiny capillaries in the human body's sweat glands break open, thus mixing blood with sweat. This produces extreme weakness and shock.

What kinds of things might have caused this for Jesus?

- Fear of the torture?
- The sinless One becoming sin?
- Life Himself dying?

- Being separated from the Father?
- Drinking from the cup of wrath?

Absolutely, all of these and so many more would cause Jesus extreme anguish as we see in His prayers while in the garden.

He went a little farther and fell on His face, and prayed, saying, "O My Father, if it is possible, let this cup pass from Me; nevertheless, not as I will, but as You will" (Matthew 26:39).

He went away and prayed, saying, "O My Father, if this cup cannot pass away from Me unless I drink it, Your will be done" (Matthew 26:42).

So He left them, went away again, and prayed the third time, saying the same words (Matthew 26:44).

What is this "cup" that Jesus is referring to?

For in the hand of the Lord there is a cup, and the wine is red; it is fully mixed, and He pours it out (Psalm 75:8).

For thus says the Lord God of Israel to me: "Take this wine cup of fury from My hand, and cause all the nations, to whom I send you, to drink it. And they will drink and stagger and go mad" (Jeremiah 25:15-16).

You will be filled with drunkenness and sorrow, the cup of horror and desolation (Ezekiel 23:33).

You who have drunk at the hand of the Lord the cup of His fury; you have drunk the dregs of the cup of trembling (Isaiah 51:17).

In the garden, Jesus is looking at the cup of wrath. This is the cup He has come to save us from. No wonder His soul is overwhelmed with sorrow to the point of death!

Remember, Jesus said, *"I have a baptism to be baptized with, and how great is my distress until it is accomplished!"* (Luke 12:50 ESV). This cup, this baptism of wrath, is what He was referring to.

The Lord thoroughly understood the Scriptures as He had dictated them to the disciples. He totally, with perfect insight, understood the wrath of God. Unlike any man before Him, He knew what the suffering entailed. The cup of wrath was the reason He came.

To destroy the work of the devil (see 1 John 3:8), this cup was more than just a common scourging or crucifixion, as horrific as those are; it was the infilling of the cup of wrath directly from the Father because of willful sin. None of God's children had ever experienced that cup before. Jesus was preparing to accept the eternal wrath and judgment of the Almighty God containing Hell's blazing fire. It was weightier than we can even begin to fathom.

Jonathan Edwards said that Jesus would endure the "very pains of hell" not *after* the cross but *on* the cross.

Why did Jesus drink this cup? *"He himself shall also drink of the wine of the wrath of God, which is poured out full strength into the cup of His indignation. He shall be tormented with fire and brimstone in the presence of the holy angels and in the presence of the Lamb"* (Rev. 14:10).

This understanding of the cup of wrath was given to Jesus as a Man in a human body before He was given over to His enemies. Jesus endured extreme torture in His soul before the whip, the crown of thorns, the nails, the lack of oxygen, or His heart exploding. Jesus accepted the suffering of the cup of wrath because He wanted something.

We have to understand—Jesus could have said "No."

If He had, all people would live eternally in Hell because all people have sinned (see Rom. 3:23). Instead, Jesus looked into the cup and remembered the reason why He had agreed to be born in the first place. He saw the only way for us to be reconciled to the Father. He was willing to do what no false god would ever do. Jesus agreed to drink that cup for me! It was the only way that I wouldn't have to drink it myself. Jesus wanted me to be with Him eternally.

Because of sin, God the Father left the planet. He cannot dwell in the unholiness of our presence. On our own, we would never be able to reconcile ourselves to God. To save us, Jesus had to throw Himself in front of the Father's eternal wrath! He is the perfect sacrifice, the slain Lamb of God that everyone has been waiting for since Adam and Eve. His holy blood covers us. He became a propitiation, the substitution, the atonement and payment for our sin. His sacrifice averted wrath from us (see Rom. 3:25; Heb. 2:17; 1 John 2:1-2; 4:10).

The unimaginable stress and dread of this cup pressed the sweat blood out of Jesus' body. And He willingly drank it so that I could spend eternity with Him! Not only was mankind torturing Jesus, Satan and all his demons had a legal right to attack Him. And there was no protection over Jesus from His Father or the mighty angels that He commanded. Jesus was alone.

On the cross, Christ suffered more than we will ever understand. He bled profusely from the scourging, the spikes tortured the nerves in His hands and feet, the crown of thorns pierced into His temples, all of His joints were dislocated, He writhed against the cross in pain, He thirsted, He struggled to breath, He was mocked and shamed, He forgave the ones He had created out of His great love, and He watched the pain in the eyes of His loved ones. *He was excruciatingly separated from His Father and the Holy Spirit.*

The people couldn't see it, but wave after wave of the Father's furious wrath was poured out onto the perfect Lamb of God who took away the sins of the world (see Isa. 53:5).

Unimaginable! The great Father in Heaven, pouring out over His innocent Son the cup of wrath that began filling with the first sin from the Garden of Eden. He poured it all onto our Savior, in its entirety, and with all of its righteous judgment. There is so much more going on at the cross than just mere evil men and the Devil punishing Jesus. Jesus didn't submit so that the Devil's wrath could be released upon Him, even though it was. Jesus submitted to the Holy One. And Jesus took every drop of the cup of wrath from His Father and took it to Hell. He drank it all so that the people He loves would have a way to be with the Father.

He cried out: *"My God, My God, why have You forsaken Me?"* (Matt. 27:46).

The penalty of sin is separation from God. God forsaking God has never been done. Satan could have never seen it coming; it dumbfounded him. The three—Father, Son, and Spirit—had always been one. Satan didn't realize that there was a love so deep for mankind that God would not let Satan have us. This love was so motivating and unmovable that it shook the foundations of what even Satan had known of God. It was unthinkable, unmeasured, unimaginable. It was, actually *is*, a holy reckless love.

The sweet cross produced victory! The perfect plan God described from the very beginning (see Gen. 3:15).

Jesus took all the punishing and annihilating sin upon Himself and separated it from us so that it would no longer separate us from the Father. Satan had no hold on Jesus because Jesus had never sinned. His holy body, soul, and spirit could not be held in Hell. The very thing that Satan had counted on using to capture us in Hell forever, the wrath of God, is the very thing that Jesus used to save us. Jesus won!

- He destroyed the work of the devil (see 1 John 3:8).

- He disarmed and triumphed over powers and princi-
  palities (see Col. 2:15).

From the cross, Jesus proclaimed an eternal truth and sentence. *"It is finished!"* (John 19:30). Meaning that it is forever and will remain forever finished.

At the cross, it has been medically proven that Jesus' heart ruptured, or broke. This is technically what killed Him. Spiritually, the cup of wrath broke His heart. At that moment, the Bible says the curtain of the temple was torn from top to bottom (see Matt. 27:51). This tearing was not merely the veil in the earthly Holy of Holies. This was the veil in Heaven that separated God from us. The rupture in the heart of Jesus reconciled us to God.

The enemy was defeated. Death was defeated. Jesus made a way where there was no way. He reconciled men to God.

RESCUED AT THE CROSS

We need the power of the cross! Whenever the cross is preached, the power of God is present. Wherever the cross is preached, disciples are commissioned.

> *For the message of the cross is foolishness to those who are perishing, but to us who are being saved it is the power of God* (1 Corinthians 1:18).

> *And whoever does not bear his cross and come after Me cannot be My disciple* (Luke 14:27).

When I study the cross I find provision and power to accomplish the good things that Jesus has prepared for me. When I preach the cross I find disciples who need to understand that He desires us to defeat the enemy in the same way that He did. The cross is not about mere endurance of torture or pain. The cross is about using the power and plan of God to succeed. It is to reconcile ourselves and others to Jesus!

Let me share a personal vision that helped me understand this. It started as I suddenly arrived at the foot of the cross. I knew immediately where I was and I instantly felt scared. It was hot and the air was charged with a dread and unspeakable doom. The air had a bad taste to it as if sulfur was all around. In addition, there was so much hatred surrounding me. I knew it would overtake me. I was *very* afraid.

The noise was deafening and very hectic as everyone was shouting and angry. There were people pressing in everywhere. I had spiritual eyes and I could see the multitudes of demons everywhere. Some of them were very large. They were all there watching, hissing, and taunting Jesus.

When I looked at the cross, I realized I was so close to it that I could have touched it. I had a center stage location for what I am about to share.

I felt the power of the cross. It was taking on the qualities of the area. The cross today is a symbol of victory, but when I stood underneath it, the piece of wood was turning into hatred, fear, and agony. It was deplorable and hideous and symbolized control and manipulation. He was nailed, not just to a piece of wood, but it was as if He was grafted into all of the terribleness the cross had absorbed. It was surreal to actually see Jesus was hanging on the cross and suffering. It was all very scary. Looking up from the bottom of the cross, I could not see Him so I stepped back many steps until I could look into His eyes. I passed a lot of demons but none of them were interested in me. They were watching and reveling in the suffering of Jesus.

I desperately needed Jesus to see me because He was the only safe thing around. It was my hope to bring a level of comfort to Him, or maybe to bring a level of comfort to me. The more I looked upon Him, the more distraught I became. I supernaturally understood that He was suffering more than anyone ever had or ever would.

I felt many emotions inside of me. My whole body physically hurt as if I had been in a car accident because the Creator was dying right in front of me. I just wanted to throw up! I was surrounded by great fear, confusion, and an ever-present evil. I couldn't stop wailing and shaking as the torture of Jesus was too much to bear even though I was only an onlooker. Although I didn't feel the physical pain He was suffering, I finally began to truly realize what salvation really meant and a part of that cross became mine.

As soon as I knew that He could see me, I shook my head "no." I wanted Him to know that I was not worth it. I felt that all of us put together were not worth the amount of pain and suffering He was enduring. I wanted Jesus to do something that He has never done nor will ever do. I wanted God to quit. I wanted Him to throw in the towel on me and on all of us. I wanted Him to take His perfection to the safety of His heavenly home. I knew that many people would never appreciate His sacrifice and would never be with Him.

As I looked at Him, I knew that He understood my heart. He understood that I had a grasp for the debt of my sin and of sin in general. Sin, the great separator. With everything in me, I began to hate sin. I was consumed with the understanding of how powerful sin is and that, unless I hated it, I would continue to allow it in my life. My sin had put Jesus on the cross. The sickness that I felt was because of the reality that He had taken *my* place. I should be the one to suffer and pay, not the perfect One. I was afraid because the reality of the price was too much to believe and I could never begin to pay the terrible price. I stayed at the cross out of the deep love I saw Jesus spending for all of us and the revelation His love opened to me. Never had anyone loved more!

In that moment, I felt abounding love surround me. I felt safe in a way that I have never felt before. As my eyes looked at Jesus, He began to nod His head as if to tell me "yes."

Suddenly, I realized I was in the arms of Father God. He was at the cross right beside me. The Father scooped me up and raced me away from the cross as I cried out that I was not worthy and it was not right for Jesus to take my place. I reached my hands out over the shoulder of God the Father to reach for Jesus. Jesus wanted me to leave quickly.

The Father crossed the darkness of the universe and set me down in a beautiful meadow under a very large tree. At first it seemed silent, compared to the wailing at the cross. But then I realized there was a rhythmic noise. It was Him. I could hear Jesus breathing. His breath was still pouring out life, but the rhythm was slowing.

The Father was so thankful that I was safe. He cupped His right hand on the left side my face and told me to stay there. As I looked at Him I mistook Him for Jesus. That made Him smile. Jesus had told us that He is the exact replication of the Father (see John 14:9). It seems silly to say this, but it is true. Jesus looks like His Father.

The Father raced back to the cross. Although I was in a safe place, I knew that Jesus was hanging on that cross dying. I didn't know which was worse—being at the cross watching Jesus die or waiting in this place knowing He was dying but not being with Him. I realized that I loved Jesus more than ever. There wasn't anything that I wouldn't do for Him. I listened to the rhythm of His breathing as if my life depended on it.

I thought about going back to Him but two angels abruptly appeared under the tree to remind me that I was commanded by the Father to stay put. I realized that *everything* God tells us really is a command. I instantly regretted that I had even considered leaving the tree. I understood that entertaining thoughts that are against God is sin. I had a new thought pattern. I hated sin. I repented immediately.

I asked the angels what the Father was doing. They looked puzzled and explained that He was at the cross rescuing the ones Jesus loves—the ones who love Him back.

I asked them why they didn't go to help the Father. I promised that I would stay put so other souls could be saved. They explained that only God can rescue people. Jesus was on the cross and the Father was moving as many as would repent to Jesus away from sin. They explained that they were mere angels. They had no power to rescue men. Then they made it clear that they did not want to talk so they too could listen to His breathing.

At that moment a deep hurt in my soul ached more than anything I can explain with my vocabulary. I listened as Jesus took His last breath and everything stopped. Life died.

I gasped and thought, "*Oh no*, the Savior is dead!" There was silence. There had never been silence like this before. Time as we knew it had stopped because the Savior had stopped breathing but we still had to continue. Neither I nor the angels knew what to do as we waited in the silence.

Suddenly, a man like wind came and handed me a gem. He was stunning in His appearance. He is impossible to describe as there is no comparison. The wind had a form but you had to look with eyes of faith to see Him. It felt as if I was peering into a promise with the security of an answer. Like a promised man made from the wind of faith. I knew somehow that the material He was made out of was like the breath of God. He liked my thoughts about Him and smiled at me. Then I could see Jesus. He smiled just like Jesus! I knew that He loved me so very much and had a special attraction to my personality. I felt as if He totally understands me and He really likes me.

The gem He gave me was mystical. I instinctively knew that it was the most costly, rare, and beautiful treasure I would ever have. It was a tear-shaped drop filled with something alive. It danced inside like a flame of fire. Each swirl of movement seemingly more spectacular than the last. It had the colors of the rainbow inside, and even more colors than that.

The man of wind closed my hand around the gem and filled me with something like fire in my heart. Then He was gone, swirling away in a gust of wind, leaving me breathless with wonder.

I tried to process this but I was struggling because it all happened so quickly. I asked the angels, "Who was the wind?" But before they could answer, I knew and immediately added, "That was the Holy Spirit?!" The angels nodded.

I peeked inside my closed fist at the gem. I wasn't sure what the Holy Spirit had given me. But as quickly as I thought the question, I had the answer. This was a drop of blood from Jesus. It was the cost for my sins. I closed my fist tighter. With this knowledge, my heart burned hotter.

I understood that Jesus had purchased me for the Father with His innocent shed blood. The Godhead was hard at work together. The three of them had separated themselves one from another and all three were playing a part for the ones They love. I was undone. Tears streamed down my face.

I asked the angels, "What do I do with it?" They looked at me and I knew they could not tell me what to do. The choice was only mine. Somehow goodwill came through their eyes and gave me strength to think clearly. They were really for me. I understood they knew what I should do and they were praying for me.

I thought several things:

- Show it off so that others could see I am valuable.
- Find a hiding place to bury it.
- Keep it in my pocket.
- Create a piece of jewelry.

All of these sound silly now, but at the time none of them seemed safe enough for this invaluable treasure. It could be stolen, misplaced, lost, or damaged. I began to question. What do you do with the drop of blood that makes sure you won't die? I prayed, "Father, help me, what should I do?"

The answer came right away. I immediately swallowed the gem! It instantly broke inside of me. All of the life inside of the gem of blood shattered into a million pieces never to be put back together again. At the same time my blood opened to swallow the lifeblood that was shattered. His crucifixion made me like Him. My heart was now totally engulfed in an all-consuming fire.

As I stood in the meadow with this new heart of fire, my life changed. I looked at the angels who were smiling and nodding. I realized that my life would be forever different because of the love of the Trinity. I stood with a new knowledge that God is good. He can *never* be the bad guy and His plan *always* works; it is perfect.

I had never known my value until it was shown to me from God's perspective. It is beyond understanding that the King desires us to be with Him so much that He was willing to pay a ridiculous and unimaginable price to make that happen. When I realized my value to His plan, my whole being rejoiced. For the first time, I fully embraced what it meant to be without the weight of sin. It was stunning and transforming.

I came out of the vision amazed! I was changed but I had so many questions. I hungered to study the power of the cross and the shed blood of Jesus. I desired to manifest that heavenly sinless walk in my everyday life. I knew that Jesus drank a cup of wrath and I drank a drop of His blood, which meant I had His power. The struggle is using that power.

His Love

The cross is where we begin to grasp His love for us. Without Jesus, we will drink from the cup of wrath (see Matt. 26:29). However, for those who accept Jesus as Savior, the cup of wrath has been emptied by the slain

Lamb. The Scriptures say that we shall overcome by the blood of the Lamb and by our testimony (see Rev. 12:11).

The Father, Jesus, and the Holy Spirit want us with Them. The *choice* is ours. Choose wisely.

ABOUT LAURIE A. DITTO

Laurie travels around the world sharing her testimonies of Heaven and Hell to reach people for Jesus. As director of *My Father's Reputation,* she trains people in the prophetic. Laurie and her husband, Mike, have been married for 35 years. Their greatest delights are their children and grandchildren.

OTHER BOOKS BY LAURIE A. DITTO

Go. Tell Others About Me

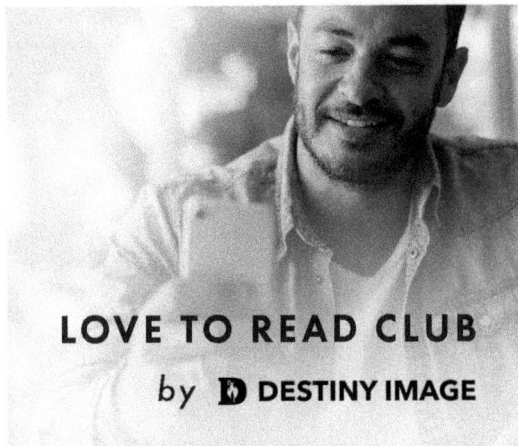

www.ingramcontent.com/pod-product-compliance
Lightning Source LLC
Chambersburg PA
CBHW070838100426
42813CB00003B/661